THE
NEW YORK PUBLIC LIBRARY
INCREDIBLE EARTH

A Book of Answers for Kids

Ann-Jeanette Campbell
and
Ronald Rood

Illustrated by
Jessica Wolk-Stanley

D0002766

A Stonesong Press Book

John Wiley & Sons, Inc.
New York • Chichester • Brisbane • Toronto • Singapore

To the students, staff, and families of P.S. 39.
—*A. J. C.*

To the students and teachers at The Medill School in Lancaster, Ohio.
—*R. R.*

This text is printed on acid-free paper.

Copyright © 1996 by The New York Public Library and The Stonesong Press, Inc.
Illustrations copyright © 1996 by The Stonesong Press, Inc.
Published by John Wiley & Sons, Inc.

Library of Congress Cataloging-in-Publication Data

Campbell, Ann-Jeanette, and Rood, Ronald N.
    The New York Public Library Incredible Earth : a book of answers for kids /
[Ann-Jeanette Campbell and Ron Rood].
        p. cm. — (The New York Public Library answer books for kids series)
    "A Stonesong Press book."
    Includes index.
    Summary: questions and answers on such topics as rocks and minerals, fossils, oceans, seasons, earthquakes, and volcanoes.
    ISBN 0-471-14497-5 (pbk. : alk. paper)
    1. Earth sciences—Miscellanea—Juvenile literature.   [1. Earth sciences—Miscellanea.   2. Questions and answers.]   I. Title.   II. Series
    QE53.R66   1996
    550—dc20   96-22112

Printed in the United States of America

10 9 8 7 6 5 4 3 2 1

Contents

INTRODUCTION

Have you ever wondered how the Earth began, why trees are shaped the way they are, or why the ocean is blue? Maybe you'd like to know what holds the air, soil, and ocean together in one clump we call the Earth?

Questions like these bring millions of people to the New York Public Library—and other libraries across the country—every day. Now you can have the answers at your fingertips.

In **The New York Public Library Incredible Earth**, you'll find the answers to some of the most commonly asked questions about how the Earth began, how life began, what's inside the Earth, why volcanoes and earthquakes happen, and much more. The easy question/answer format allows you to look up one question at a time or read a whole chapter at once. You'll also find fascinating stories about fossils, devastating earthquakes, and wild weather, to name just a few of the wonders of our incredible earth.

The New York Public Library Incredible Earth doesn't tell you everything—we don't know everything—but within these pages are the basics of Earth Science: the simple, the complex, the amazing, the common, and the extraordinary ways in which the world works.

The New York Public Library and other libraries all over the country have shelves, and computers, filled with facts to help you learn. It is our hope that this book will encourage you to investigate the libraries in your own town. Perhaps you'll find that your questions don't yet have answers. In that case, you must piece together clues from the information available and leave the rest up to your own powers of scientific thought. Maybe your answer can be used in a future edition of this book!

How did the universe begin?

Nobody knows for sure how the universe began. Over the centuries, however, through observation, mathematics, chemistry, geology, logic, inspiration, and all other human skills, scientists have formulated theories about how the universe began.

The big bang theory is the most widely accepted of these theories. It states that the universe began some 15 or 20 billion years ago in a huge explosion—the big bang. This explosion produced all matter, energy, space, and even time. Although scientists do not know why or exactly how it happened, they generally agree that this explosion sent the matter hurtling out from its center. As the matter cooled, it formed the particles that make up everything in the universe. This was the beginning of the universe, the beginning of what would eventually become you and me and everything around us.

Will the universe last forever?

According to most scientific theories, the universe will not stay as we know it forever. Most scientists agree that the universe is still expanding as a result of the initial force of the big bang. The differences of opinion on the future depend on how much physical matter exists in the universe.

If there is enough matter (and we don't know just how much the critical amount is), the force of gravity inherent in each bit of matter will sooner or later slow and stop the outward expansion. Gravity will cause the matter to reverse its course and begin to contract. At some point, the universe will fall in upon itself.

Scientists disagree on what might happen if the universe collapses in what some call the "big crunch." Another big bang might happen and the universe might begin all over again. (Would it develop in the same way again? No one knows.) A different conclusion has the big crunch creating a massive black hole, consuming time and space just as the big bang created them.

If there is not enough matter in the universe, then there is not enough gravity to reverse the course of expansion. The universe will continue to expand and the matter will continue to cool as it grows farther and farther apart. Stars will eventually die out, leaving all matter dark, cold, and essentially dead, though always expanding.

Remember, however, that some 15 billion years have passed since the big bang. The chances of someone being around to witness the big crunch or the death of the last star are the same as anyone having seen the big bang.

Theory and Hypothesis— What's the Difference?

The two words *theory* and *hypothesis* often get mixed up. The difference between them may not seem important, but it is.

A theory is a collection of ideas or propositions proved by logic and the accumulation of facts and justifiable assumptions. Theories are held to be true, but they can, and sometimes are, proven wrong by the discovery of new information. For instance, before Christopher Columbus sailed to North America, western Europeans believed the theory that Earth was flat. Columbus's new information proved this theory to be wrong.

A hypothesis is a possible explanation arrived at by studying facts, using logic and assumption, but it is still in a formative stage. Over time, and generally through experimentation, hypotheses that are proven to be true from all we know become theories. Scientists commonly set forth a hypothesis and then go about trying to prove whether it is right or wrong. They might say, "It's an idea. Let's check it out."

What is matter?

We use the term *matter* as a general word for scientific "stuff." By matter we mean atoms, elements, particles, dust, gases, rocks, minerals, and their various combinations. The basic scientific definition of matter is something that has mass and takes up space. Using *matter* as a general word is helpful because specifically naming the components that make up the raw material of Earth or the universe would get complicated. Reading this book would be very difficult, except for a scientist. When practical or pertinent, more specific names are used and explained.

What are atoms?

Atoms are the units that make up elements, or pure subtances. Atoms are extremely tiny—it would take millions of atoms just to cover up the dot of an "i" on this page.

Atomic theory, in a very simplified summary, states that everything is made up of atoms and that there is a fixed number of different types of atoms. Different atoms make up different elements. This means that all of the atoms of a particular element, like gold or oxygen, are of the same type.

Atoms combine to make elements, and different elements combine and react with each other to form gases, liquids, and solids.

How was Earth formed?

It took a long time for the matter produced in the big bang to form galaxies, stars, and eventually Earth. Gradually, as the spinning, whirling bits of matter from the big bang flew off into space, larger and larger chunks collided with each other. These chunks drew together to form suns, planets, moons, stars, and asteroids.

About 5 billion years ago, a certain medium-size star exploded into existence. Its matter collapsed on itself, causing incredible pressure and heat. This became our Sun. The gravitational energy around the newly formed Sun attracted nearby chunks of matter. These began to **orbit** the big star, or to travel in a circular path around it. Earth was one of those collections of matter. At that time it was a hot ball of thick dust, **mineral** particles, and gas—not what we imagine when we use the word Earth.

How did Earth form from gases, dust clouds, and chunks of material?

All of this matter was drawn together by **gravity**, or the force of attraction between two objects. Gravity is, of course, what usually keeps your feet on the ground and makes you fall when you trip over your shoelaces. Scientists are not exactly sure how the matter came together to form a solid Earth. One theory is that the heavier particles, metals like iron and nickel, sank to the center, while lighter material remained on the outside. Another theory is that the heaviest particles clumped together first, then attracted the lighter material. Either way, this whirling clump of matter was held in orbit by the strength of the Sun's gravity.

What stops Earth from crashing into the Sun if the Sun's gravitational force is so strong?

When Earth formed, it created its own gravitational force, enhanced by spinning, or **rotating**. This kept the collected material together. Without the Sun's gravity, Earth would go spinning off into space, but without Earth's own gravity in conjunction with the gravitational force from other planets, it would be drawn into the Sun. So, while the Sun pulls Earth toward it, the cumulative gravity of Earth and the other planets keeps it in its orbit around the Sun. Think of it as a multiple tug-of-war.

When did Earth become Earth?

Scientists date the start of Earth about 4.5 billion years ago, perhaps even more. Probably the most fascinating fact about the whole universe is that it is always changing, always becoming something new. Changes can happen over billions of years—so slowly we don't see them—or they can happen in a flash, like the explosion of a star. From the start, Earth has been in a state of flux, always changing, always becoming something slightly different from what it was.

How fast does Earth travel in its orbit around the Sun?

Earth speeds along at an average of 66,600 miles (107,000 kilometers) per hour. That's 1,100 miles (1,800 kilometers) every minute, or 18.5 miles (29.8 kilometers) every second. Because you are on Earth, you are traveling at the same speed.

Why does Earth rotate?

Everything in the universe is constantly moving. Matter from the big bang is still moving outward from the center of the universe. Gases and materials spun off from the original explosion in eddies, like the whirlpools you can make in water by swirling your hand in a circle. Unless these celestial bodies are stopped, by crashing into another body, for instance, they continue to turn while they travel through space. The same is true of Earth—it was rotating as it formed and has not stopped.

How Long Is Four Billion Years?

It is not easy to get an idea of what a billion years means. Obviously, it is a long period of time, but it is tough to imagine. One way to try to get a grasp on long periods of time is to compare them to more familiar periods of time. Let's look at spans of time leading back to four billion years ago.

The United States of America didn't exist four hundred (400) years ago.

The great pyramids of Egypt were built a little over four thousand (4,000) years ago.

Humans did not inhabit the Americas until forty thousand (40,000) years ago.

Humans had not finished evolving from apes four hundred thousand (400,000) years ago.

Apes began to evolve into human species some four million (4,000,000) years ago.

The Rocky Mountains in the United States were created at least forty million (40,000,000) years ago.

The first invertebrates (creatures without spines) crawled from the water onto land some four hundred million (400,000,000) years ago.

More than four billion (4,000,000,000) years ago, a chunk of space debris became Earth.

Such lengths of time still aren't easy to imagine!

Why is Earth always tilted in mounted globes?

Earth's **axis**—the imaginary line around which Earth rotates—tilts about 23.5° from an upright, or vertical, position relative to the Sun. Globes show this tilt so that you can picture the way Earth spins as it revolves around the Sun.

Earth's axis tilts at an angle of 23.5° in relation to its orbit of the Sun.

Does Earth's axis always stay in the same place?

Gravity is a mighty force. The combined gravity of the Sun and Moon actually make Earth's axis change the angle of rotation slightly. The change in angle is called precession. If you extended the imaginary line of the axis into the atmosphere, the axis would appear to draw a sweeping cone shape in the air over the course of 26,000 years. Speeded up, precession would make Earth look a bit like a spinning top that was wobbling. The effect of precession on each of us, however, is unnoticeable, as it happens so slowly.

Why does Earth seem to stand still while the Sun moves across the sky?

Earth is moving around the Sun at about 1,100 miles (1,800 kilometers) a minute, but there isn't anything close by to show us how fast we're moving. Traveling in a car, you see nearby bushes and buildings rushing by, but mountains in the distance don't seem to move at all. If we had other **satellites** (objects orbiting Earth) close by along the route of Earth's orbit, we'd see how fast we were going. But the stars are like the mountains, too far away to help us judge our speed. While Earth revolves around the Sun, it also rotates on its own axis, one rotation

You should never look directly at the Sun. The light is so powerful that it could damage your eyes.

every 24 hours. We don't feel either of these movements because we move right along with Earth.

If Earth is constantly revolving and rotating, why don't we fly off into space?

Good old gravity keeps our feet on the ground. Earth's gravitational force holds us—and everything else—on the planet. That's why getting off the ground in an airplane or a space rocket takes an enormous amount of power. Anything trying to leave Earth has to overcome the planet's gravitational pull.

On the average, you take a breath every 6 seconds. With every breath, you—and Earth—have gone approximately 100 miles (180 kilometers).

Is sunshine the same all over Earth?

No. Because Earth is spherical, the Sun's rays hit the **equator** (the imaginary line separating the northern and southern halves of Earth) directly and the rest of Earth at various angles. Because the equator receives the most direct sunlight all year, the equatorial regions have a relatively consistent, temperate climate. Direct rays are the shortest and strongest, which is why the climate at the equator is generally hot. Angled rays are longer and weaker, so Earth's North and South Poles remain cold.

Are areas near the equator always warm?

Average temperatures of equatorial regions tend to be warmer than in areas farther away from the equator. The top of Mount Kenya, however, while near the equator in East Africa, is covered in snow all year around—just like the North and South Poles. This is because **elevation** (height above sea level) is a factor in determining temperature. The higher the elevation of a place, the colder it will be, even if it is near the equator.

Why are summer days longer than winter days?

It's the same reason that Earth has seasons: because Earth's axis is tilted in relation to the Sun. If the axis were straight up and down, different parts of the world would still have different lengths of daylight and darkness, but they would remain constant throughout the year.

When the Northern **Hemisphere**, or half, of Earth is tilted toward the Sun, the Sun's rays hit it more directly.

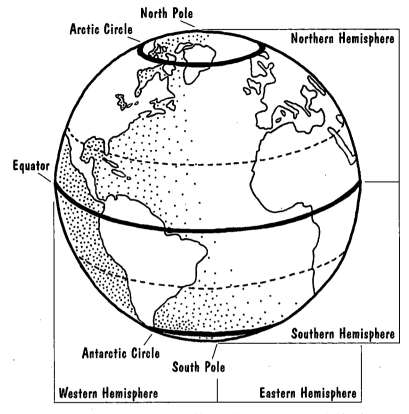

Earth is divided into two sets of hemispheres. The equator divides the
Northern and Southern Hemispheres. The Eastern and Western Hemispheres
are divided by the 0° meridian, or the prime meridian, on one side of the globe
and the 180° meridian on the other (both not shown). The two dotted lines
show the tropics of Cancer (north of the equator) and Capricorn (south of the
equator). Within these two imaginary lines the Sun's rays are strongest.

The more direct—and therefore warmer—sunshine creates summer in the Northern Hemisphere. The tilt of Earth
also makes the Northern Hemisphere experience longer
days during this time, and the Sun appears to pass higher
in the sky. Six months later, Earth has moved halfway
through its orbit, and the Southern Hemisphere is tilted
toward the Sun. This means it is summer in the Southern
Hemisphere and winter in the Northern Hemisphere.

You can see the change in the angle of the Sun very
gradually over the course of several months. In the
Northern Hemisphere, the Sun climbs higher in the sky

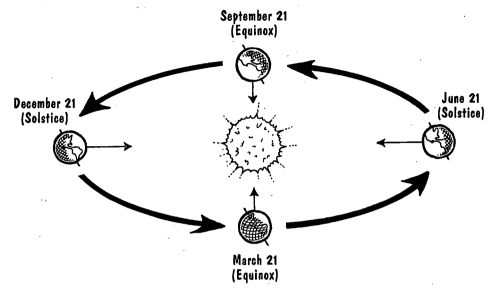

September 21
(Equinox)

December 21
(Solstice)

June 21
(Solstice)

March 21
(Equinox)

This drawing shows how Earth's tilt gives us seasons. The hemisphere tilted away from the Sun experiences winter, while the hemisphere tilted toward the Sun has summer.

each day as summer approaches, until one day—on or about June 21—it seems to stop getting higher. After that, it drops lower each day as winter comes closer. Then it stops—on about December 21—and begins to climb higher again. June 21 is called the **summer solstice**, or "summer sun standing still"; December 21 is the **winter solstice**, or "winter sun standing still." In the Southern Hemisphere, summer and winter are reversed.

What are the North and South Poles?

Earth actually has two north and two south poles. The geographic North and South Poles are the northern and southern points of Earth's axis. The magnetic north and south poles mark the strongest points of Earth's magnetic field. While near each other, the two northern poles and the two southern poles are in different spots.

Finding the Poles

Many explorers tried—and failed—to find the exact location of the geographic North and South Poles. Weather conditions at the poles made the discovery difficult. The North Pole is located in the Arctic Ocean, making it especially hard to find amid the shifting ice and crevasses. Robert Peary and Matthew Henson finally reached it in 1909. In 1911, Roald A. Amundsen found the South Pole on the frozen continent of Antarctica.

What is Earth's magnetic field?

You have probably experimented with magnets and have seen for yourself how they attract and repel other magnetic metals. Certain metals—iron, cobalt, and nickel—contain electronically charged atoms that arrange themselves to produce two forces, called a positive force and a negative force, at either end of their surface. A positive force attracts a negative force and repels a positive force. These charged metals are magnets.

Earth itself has a magnetic field. The cause of Earth's magnetic field is not fully understood, but seems to be a result of the metals within its core. The core acts something like a huge magnet, as if a big bar magnet were inside Earth. The strongest points of the magnetic field—called poles— are at the north and south. The north pole is the positive pole and the south pole is the negative pole. Opposite poles attract and like poles repel each other, so a compass with a magnetized needle will always swing its negative point (pole) to the north.

How does a compass work?

When two magnets are placed near each other, the north pole of one magnet is attracted to the south pole of the other. This happens even if one magnet is huge, like Earth, and the other magnet is small, like a compass needle. The compass needle swings on a central pivot, lining up in a north-south direction. Once you find north, you can figure out the other directions.

Does a compass always point to magnetic north?

A compass may be influenced by nearby metallic objects: an automobile, the iron girders of a bridge, underground deposits of iron or nickel, or high-powered electrical lines. This is known as compass deviation. These other objects will skew the compass needle from pointing directly north, so you must take your environment into account when using a compass.

Why is it so cold at the North and South Poles?

The poles never face the Sun directly. The Sun's rays always hit the poles at an angle, which decreases their strength.

Imagine a pin striking a balloon. If the pin hits the balloon at an angle, it will likely glance off the surface without the strength to break it. But if the pin hits the balloon squarely—well, try it. The direct pinprick has much more force than the angled one.

How big is Earth?

Measured at the equator, Earth is 7,926 miles (12,756 kilometers) in **diameter**, or the distance through the center. Measured from geographic pole to pole, Earth is 7,900 miles (12,714 kilometers) in diameter. The measurements

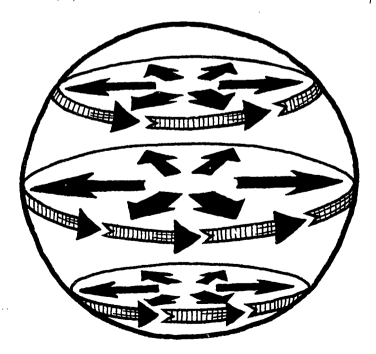

Earth bulges slightly at the equator—it is not a perfect sphere. This is because centrifugal force created by its rotation pushes out the material at Earth's center.

differ because Earth is not a true sphere. The pressure of rotation makes Earth bulge slightly in the middle so that it is shaped more like a tangerine than a tennis ball. In **circumference**, or the distance around the middle, Earth is 24,902 miles (40,075 kilometers) at the equator.

How far is Earth from the Sun?

Earth averages a distance of 93 million miles (150 million kilometers) from the Sun. That is an average because the path of Earth's orbit is not a circle. It is a stretched-out circle, or oval, called an **ellipse**.

Why isn't Earth's orbit a circle?

An object with enough speed will try to break the gravitational force of the body it orbits. The relationship between the Sun's gravitational pull and Earth's speed creates Earth's elliptical, rather than circular, orbit. Earth's orbit is not as exaggerated as it is usually drawn. At its farthest point of orbit, about July 6, Earth is 95 million miles (153 million kilometers) away from the Sun. At its closest point, about January 3, it is 91 million miles (146 million kilometers) away.

What was Earth like when it first formed?

At first Earth was just a collection of matter—a hot ball of dust, mineral particles, and gases. The matter gradually cooled to create planet Earth. Although Earth cooled, its temperatures still ranged beyond 2,700° Fahrenheit (1,000° Celsius). This was cool enough to produce a relatively delicate surface of **basalt** covering the molten rock within. Volcanic eruptions and careening asteroids frequently shattered the surface, but it would form again each time.

There was no **atmosphere**, or layer of gases, around Earth to speak of at the beginning. The first atmosphere was created about 4.2 billion years ago. Volcanic eruptions and asteroids hitting Earth released carbon dioxide, nitrogen, water vapor, ammonia, and methane, plus many other gases from the material within Earth. These gases were held in place by Earth's gravity, creating our first atmosphere. It was not a healthy atmosphere by today's standards, but it was enough to set life in motion.

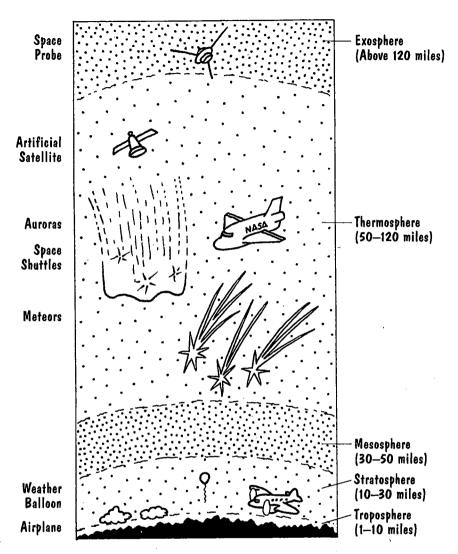

Space Probe

Artificial Satellite

Auroras

Space Shuttles

Meteors

Weather Balloon

Airplane

Exosphere
(Above 120 miles)

Thermosphere
(50–120 miles)

Mesosphere
(30–50 miles)

Stratosphere
(10–30 miles)

Troposphere
(1–10 miles)

Earth's atmosphere has five main layers. Living things can only breathe below the stratosphere because the air gets too thin farther from the surface.

What is Earth's atmosphere like now?

Dry air that we breathe is composed mostly of nitrogen and oxygen, with trace amounts of argon, carbon dioxide, neon, helium, krypton, xenon, hydrogen, ozone, nitrous oxide, and methane. Nitrogen makes up 78 percent of the air; oxygen, 21 percent; and argon, is just under 1 percent. The remainder consists of traces of the other elements. Moisture, or water vapor, in the air runs from 0 percent over desert regions to 4 percent over parts of the tropics.

What are the layers of the atmosphere called?

More than three-quarters of our air is contained in the 10 miles (16 kilometers) of the atmosphere nearest Earth's surface. This layer is called the troposphere. This first layer is where clouds and weather occur. The stratosphere above it extends 30 miles (48 kilometers) from the surface of Earth. Sometimes airplanes fly in the lowest part of the stratosphere to avoid bad weather in the troposphere. From 30 to 50 miles (48 to 80 kilometers) is the mesosphere, and after that the thermosphere, which stretches up to 120 miles (200 kilometers) into the atmosphere. After the thermosphere comes space, which we call the exosphere. The layers are defined by their range of temperature.

What does Earth's atmosphere do?

The layer of atmosphere around Earth is relatively thin, proportionately about the same as the skin around an orange. This layer is very important, however, because its gases absorb most of the harmful rays of the Sun while letting through sunlight for energy and warmth. Without the atmosphere, living things would be burned by the strong sunshine. Scientists have suggested that early forms of life developed under about 30 feet (10 meters) of water to avoid being destroyed by the Sun. Green plants in the oceans very gradually added oxygen to the atmosphere. As the gases in Earth's atmosphere increased, living things were shielded from some of the Sun's dangerous rays and eventually could exist on land as well as underwater.

How did Earth become more like it is now?

Earth continued to cool and solidify. Water vapor condensed into water, which covered Earth's surface. A thin layer of basalt and granite (a very hard type of rock) formed a permanent crust under the ocean. Land masses known as **greenstone belts**, made mostly of granite, formed the ancient cores of our modern continents. These belts also contained most of the world's deposits of gold.

Continental shields, large, low areas of stable rock in Earth's crust, were created by the greenstone granite colliding to form what is called **basement rock**. This became the foundation of the continents. Rocks from this time are currently exposed—and virtually unchanged—in North America, Africa, and Australia.

What is the origin of the Moon?

Scientists have been thinking about this question for a long time. They began by keeping track of the Moon's motions, then taking photographs of the Moon's surface, sending astronauts to study it, and analyzing its rocks. There is not enough evidence, however, to prove any single one hypothesis that explains the Moon's origin. In astronomy, just as in any branch of science, scientists revise and update their explanations for things as new data is collected. Sometimes they collect enough information to say for sure that one hypothesis is *not* true—or less likely than the others.

What are the likely hypotheses of the Moon's formation?

One possibility suggested by scientists is called the fission hypothesis. It states that early in its formation Earth was spinning so quickly that a glob of molten material was thrown off into space. The molten rock was kept in orbit by Earth's gravity and gradually cooled. The second idea is called the capture hypothesis, in which a body of material from far off in space came close enough to be grabbed by Earth's gravity. A combination of the two hypotheses is most likely: An asteroid's impact with Earth sent matter flying into orbit, creating a ring around the planet. Over time, the matter came together to make the Moon. But, where the Moon came from is still mostly an unanswered question.

What caused the pockmarked appearance of the Moon's surface?

Many of the pockmarks are actually craters made by the impact of meteorite collisions. Others are craters made by volcanoes that may have been active many years ago. Flat places on the Moon's surface are called **mares**, after the Latin word for seas. They look like dried-up ocean floors miles in diameter.

Why does the Moon seem to have so many more craters than Earth?

The Moon's gravity is not strong enough to hold an atmosphere, so there are no winds to blow sand and dust into the craters. Without water vapor, liquid water does not create lakes and there is no plant life. With no water or vegetation to hide the Moon's surface, every detail is visible.

A person weighing 100 pounds (45 kilograms) on Earth would weigh one-sixth as much on the Moon—about 17 pounds (7.65 kilograms).

How does gravity hold an atmosphere?

Just as gravity holds satellites, such as the Moon, in orbit, it holds all other material: chemicals, elements, dust, water vapor. The atmosphere is made up of these things. In the absence of gravity, all matter escapes farther and farther into space.

How large is the Moon?

The Moon has a diameter of 2,160 miles (3,478 kilometers), about the driving distance between Seattle, Washington, and San Antonio, Texas. At about one-quarter the size of Earth, it is one of the biggest satellites in the solar system. Our Moon is also unusually large in comparison to its host planet. Most satellites are quite small, less than a quarter of the size of the planets which they orbit.

What is a satellite?

Most of us are familiar with the word *satellite* meaning metal objects that are **fabricated**, or made by humans—

scientific equipment sent into space to relay television signals or to spy on other countries. But the more generic definition of the term is any body in orbit around another. This includes moons as well as television signal relay stations.

How strong is the pull of the Moon's gravity?

Being smaller than Earth, the Moon does not have nearly as much gravitational pull. Astronauts walking on the Moon are able to hop on its surface as if they were on springs, covering a few feet in one step.

Without gravity, there would be no such thing as weight. The stronger the gravity, the more an object weighs.

What causes the phases of the Moon?

The Moon doesn't actually get smaller or larger during its phases. The changes we see in the Moon result from the fact that the Moon orbits Earth.

The Moon reflects the light the Sun shines on it. When the Moon passes between Earth and the Sun in its orbit, we don't see the Moon at all because the sunlight is hitting the side facing away from us. This is the phase we call the New Moon.

As the Moon's position changes in relation to Earth and the Sun, we see either less and

Newton's Laws of Motion

What we know about gravity and the motion of objects came from Sir Isaac Newton. In 1687, he published his laws of gravity and motion in his book *Principia*.

Newton's law of gravity states that every particle of matter in the universe attracts every other particle of matter in the universe. The power of a particle's gravity depends on its mass and the distance between it and the particle it is attracting.

Newton's first law of motion says that any object at rest or moving in a uniformly straight motion will stay that way until another object or force acts upon it. (Body A stays at rest until Body B disturbs it.)

The second law states that when acted upon, the object at rest will respond by moving in the same direction and with the same momentum as the force or other object (providing that no other force is at work). (When moved by Body B, Body A moves with the same momentum and in the same direction as Body B.)

Law number three describes how the object set in motion by a force will exert an equal force in the opposite direction against the force that moves it. (When Body B exerts a force on Body A, Body A in turn exerts an equal force on Body B, in the opposite direction.)

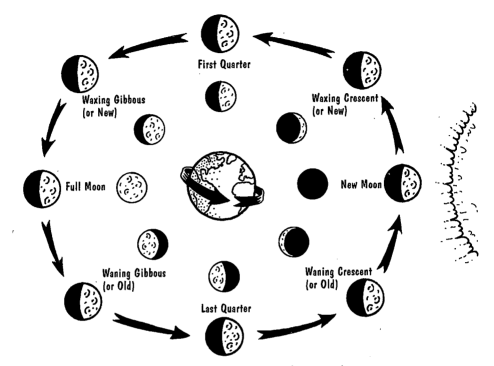

This drawing shows the positions of the Moon at various times in its orbit of Earth. The inner circle shows you how the Moon appears to a viewer on Earth at those times.

The word "month" comes from an old English word referring to the time it takes for the Moon to go through its phases.

less, or more and more, of the Moon's surface with each passing night.

When we see the whole face of the Moon bathed in sunlight, it appears round and bright, a Full Moon. Each night, as the Moon orbits, we see less and less of this lighted portion.

As the Full Moon becomes a New Moon (or **wanes**), the phases are known as Old Gibbous, Last Quarter, and Old Crescent. As the New Moon becomes a Full Moon (or **waxes**), the phases are named New Crescent, First Quarter, and New Gibbous.

How long does it take the Moon to orbit Earth?

The Moon orbits Earth once about every 27⅓ days. But a complete cycle of the Moon's phases takes about 29½ days. This is because at the same time the Moon orbits Earth, Earth orbits the Sun at a different rate, taking the Moon along with it. So, when the Moon has finished one revolution, the Sun is in a different place from where it was when the Moon began its revolution. It takes the Moon almost two extra days to reach its cycle's starting position in relation to the Sun.

Does the Moon rotate on an axis?

Yes, it does. Just like Earth, it not only orbits, but rotates.

How come we always see the same side of the Moon if it is rotating?

The Moon's rotation takes the same amount of time as its orbit, 27⅓ days. Therefore, the same side of the Moon always faces Earth.

What effect does the Moon have on Earth?

There are a lot of answers to this question as the Moon influences Earth and its inhabitants in many ways.

Perhaps the greatest effect the Moon has on Earth is to create **tides**. The relatively slight gravitational pull of the Moon pulls on Earth's large bodies of water, creating high and low tides. Water gathers where the Moon passes closest to Earth, creating high tide. Low tide

Moon Beliefs

People once believed that the Moon was more important than the Sun. They saw that daytime was light even when the Sun was hidden by clouds. They felt the Sun was not as necessary as, and, was less powerful than, the Moon.

People weren't aware that the Moon had no light of its own, but merely reflected the light of the Sun. As far as they could see, the Sun shone only when it felt like it, on nice, clear days. The Moon, however, shone in the dark, when it was needed—especially in the ages before electric lights. And the Moon didn't always show its light, suggesting its great power—not to mention the astonishing event of a solar eclipse, when the Moon took out the Sun.

Witches have always been connected with the Moon. Their ceremonies often take place according to the Moon's phases. Traditionally, not only witches, but herbalists, shamans, and apothecaries have picked certain plants only at night and only when the Moon is full or new. The date of the Christian holiday Easter is also based on the Moon's phases.

Still today, some people cite the Full Moon as the cause of madness. People feeling out of sorts are often relieved to discover there is a Full Moon. They attribute their state to the Moon's effect.

results from water leaving one area to form high tide in another.

Land does not move as easily as water, but Earth's surface rises and falls as the Moon passes over it—an inch or two in some places.

More baby animals are born during a Full Moon than at other times of the month.

Nocturnal animals are highly sensitive to the Moon's phases. Small creatures, such as mice, may be more cautious during a Full Moon since then they are more visible to their predators. Predators, such as foxes, in turn, use the nighttime shadows as cover so they aren't easily seen by their prey.

Many flowers, although open during the day, release their fragrance only at night. Some night-blooming species open only when the Moon is shining.

What is an eclipse?

Planets and moons do not give off their own light. They reflect light from a star. They also cast shadows, just like we do when we are in sunlight. An eclipse takes place when one **celestial body** passes through the shadow of another. An eclipse may be partial, with only some rays hidden, or total, when all the sun's rays are cut off. Remember, there cannot be an eclipse without **syzygy**.

Syzygy, from a Greek word meaning "yoked," or bound together, refers to the alignment of celestial bodies. Without the exact lining up of the Sun, Earth, and the Moon, there can be no eclipse of any kind: solar, lunar, or annular.

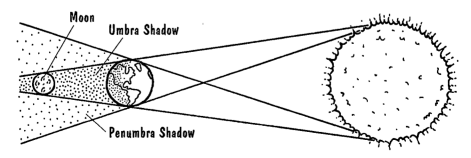

A lunar eclipse occurs when Earth blocks the Sun's light from hitting the Moon. Lunar eclipses only occur when the Moon is full, and they can be viewed without light filters or telescopes. Strong filters are necessary to view a solar eclipse.

Total Eclipse   Annular Eclipse   Partial Eclipse

These three drawings show what the Sun looks like during the different types of solar eclipses.

What is a solar eclipse?

A solar eclipse occurs when the Moon goes between Earth and the Sun, casting Earth into its shadow. Thus, the Moon blocks our view of the Sun completely for a time.

What is a lunar eclipse?

When Earth moves directly between the Sun and Moon, it casts its shadow on the Moon, blocking it from view.

What is an annular eclipse?

The Moon's orbit around Earth is elliptical, in the shape of an elongated circle. If the Moon is at its farthest point away from Earth at the time of a solar eclipse, its shadow is too short to reach Earth. And the Moon is too far away to obscure the whole Sun. The round Moon blocks all of the Sun except a bright ring of light, or **annula**, visible all around the edge of the Moon. It is an impressive event.

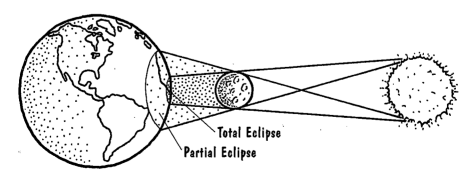

Total Eclipse
Partial Eclipse

In a solar eclipse, the Moon passes between the Sun and Earth. Viewers in the dark area see a total eclipse, while viewers in the shaded area see a partial eclipse. Because the Moon's shadow on Earth is small, viewers in some parts of the world do not see the eclipse at all.

Is the Sun's annula the same as its corona?

There is a slight difference. Both are circular rings of light from the Sun, but the annula is a ring of the Sun's surface visible during an annular eclipse. The ring-shaped corona, an everpresent bright and flaring indication of the Sun's tremendous energy, extends around the Sun. It usually cannot be seen because of the blinding brilliance of the Sun itself, but is visible during an annular eclipse. Its shooting flames of light extend thousands of miles into space.

Do eclipses have an effect on Earth life?

A partial eclipse may result only in a dimming of the Sun or Moon's light, as if a cloud had passed over. A total solar eclipse, however, may bring a dramatic change. Daytime creatures may get ready for night. Turtles, snakes, and alligators sunning themselves slip into the water. Robins and other birds begin their evening songs, while chickens and turkeys go to roost. Nocturnal animals and insects begin to stir and awake. Daytime-blooming flowers may close while their nocturnal relations start to open. Half the world, it seems, suddenly begins preparing for the night.

How long do eclipses last?

The shadow of the Moon passes relatively quickly over Earth's surface in a solar eclipse. The Sun is completely blocked out for less than 8 minutes as viewed from any one place on Earth. Lunar eclipses last longer.

How Eclipses Affect People

Eclipses are special events of a natural phenomenon which are commonly celebrated with a party-like attitude. Everyone scurries around making special boxes through which to watch the solar eclipse—because everyone knows that looking at a solar eclipse with the naked eye can cause severe visual damage, even permanent blindness. However, in ages past, when people were unaware of the natural explanations of eclipses, these unexpected events were frightening. Some people thought that a great dragon was eating the Sun. It seemed as though the world were coming to an end. People sacrificed animals, and probably each other, lit fires, threw themselves off cliffs, offered songs, prayers, and words of encouragement to the gods or the Sun itself. Don't die! And, sure enough, the Sun returned.

In a total lunar eclipse, the time when the Moon is completely blocked out may be up to 100 minutes.

Besides Earth and the Moon, what other planets and satellites are there in our solar system?

There are nine planets that revolve around our Sun. In order, from closest to the Sun to farthest from it, they are Mercury, Venus, Earth, Mars, Jupiter, Saturn, Uranus, Neptune, and Pluto. The planets and the Sun make up our solar system, along with planetary satellites, asteroids, comets, and other small interplanetary objects.

What are the planets like?

Each is unique, but they share certain qualities. All, of course, orbit the Sun, caught in its gravitational force. All are solid or partially solid and reflect light. All but two—Mercury and Venus—have at least one

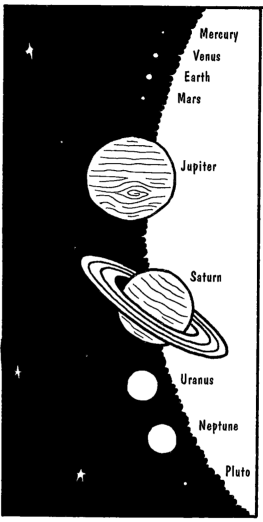

The relative sizes of the Sun and the planets in our solar system. Jupiter is the largest planet. Pluto is the smallest planet, smaller even than the Moon.

satellite, or moon, of their own. To our knowledge, none—other than Earth—has any life forms. We call the first four terrestrial planets because they share many earthlike qualities. The next four are known as Jovian planets, because they are like the planet Jupiter. (Jove is another name for Jupiter.) Jovian planets—also called gas giants—have small solid centers, but huge, thick layers of gases. Pluto is like no other planet. The planets closer to the Sun than Earth are also called the inferior planets; those farther from the Sun than Earth, including Pluto, are called the superior planets.

What is the Sun?

Our Sun is a medium-size, medium-bright star. It exploded into existence about 4.6 billion years ago, becoming the center of our solar system. Like everything in the universe, the Sun is constantly moving and changing. This is hardly noticeable, however, because we move along with it, and the changes happen over millions of years. The Sun is moving about 155 miles (249.55 kilometers) per second in the direction of 2 stars, Virgo and Hydra Centaurus, dragging our solar system with it. As with all stars, our Sun has a life expectancy. Right now, the Sun is categorized as a dwarf, a medium-mass star. It will ultimately—billions and billions of years from now—cool down and die out or become a black hole.

What are stars?

The nearest star is 4.4 light-years, or 25.872 trillion miles (41.654 trillion kilometers), away.

Stars are balls of hot **ionized** (electrically charged) gas called plasma. Their energy comes from the complex process of thermonuclear fusion, similar to nuclear bombs. Stars begin as nebulae, or clouds of gas and dust.

A nova is a star system that suddenly becomes incredibly bright and then slowly decreases in brightness again. This happens when one star gathers the material of a local star into itself. A supernova is a nova on a big scale.

Do stars remain forever?

Stars change over time. Stars like the Sun are known as red dwarfs. These are the most common class of star in our galaxy. It will spend most of its life—about 100 billion years—fusing hydrogen into helium for energy. When it has used up its hydrogen, it will swell up into a red giant and burn its helium. When its helium is gone, the star will begin to contract, through the force of self-gravity. It will then move on to become a white dwarf, which signals the beginning of its decline. Finally it dies out and becomes what is known as a black dwarf, a dead star.

The largest stars, with great mass, have shorter lives and more violent ends, sometimes becoming black holes. No one knows for sure what black holes are, but most scientists believe they occur as a result of the crush of gravity on the mass of a great star. The star collapses on itself, essentially becoming nothing but gravity, which continues to pull on anything passing by, even light! That's why it's called a black hole.

What is the Sun like?

The Sun is huge, hot, and powerful compared to Earth, although it is only a medium-size star. Its equatorial diameter measures 863,746 million miles (1,390,631 million kilometers). It has the volume of 1,333,000 Earths. The Sun's gravitational pull is almost 30 times that of Earth. The Sun also rotates once every 25 days.

Unimaginably hot, the Sun's surface temperature registers an average 9,980° Fahrenheit (5,527.6° Celsius). Write out the number 27 and put 69 zeros after it. That's how hot the Sun's core is in degrees Fahrenheit.

Does the Sun have an atmosphere?

With the Sun's gravity 27.9 times Earth's, the answer is a

Sun Myths

The Sun has frequently held an honored place in the mythologies of people. Apollo, the ancient Roman god of the Sun, rode his blazing chariot through the sky every day.

In Hopi legend, the Sun made his journey across the sky beginning and ending in the kivas, or underground ceremonial rooms, of two sister goddesses, each named Huruing Wuhti. (Huruing Wuhti means "hard-beings woman," goddess of rock, clay, minerals, and precious stones.) In the eastern kiva, he donned a gray fox coat, which stood for the dawn. In the sky, he changed to a yellow fur, for the midday. As he entered the kiva in the west, he shook a turtle shell rattle, signaling the end of the day. He then swam underwater back to the eastern kiva to begin his trek through the sky again.

The Sun was all-important to Amenhotep IV, the Egyptian pharaoh who came to power in 1379 B.C. Amenhotep established an innovative religion that worshiped only one god, instead of the usual pantheon of immortals. The one, all-powerful god was Aton, the Sun.

Most religions today do not worship the Sun, but it is an enduring symbol of power and life in religion, poetry, and literature.

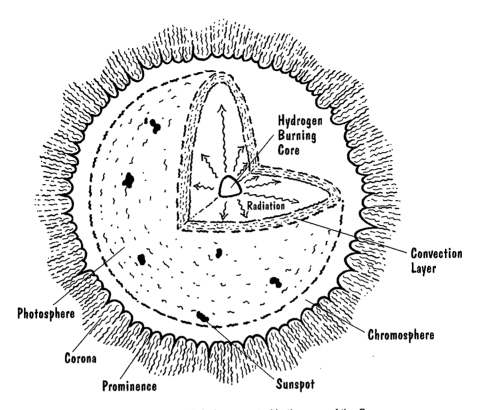

Hydrogen
Burning
Core

Radiation

Convection
Layer

Photosphere

Chromosphere

Corona

Prominence   Sunspot

The energy that produces sunlight is generated in the core of the Sun, where hydrogen is converted to helium in a nuclear reaction. The energy travels out from the core, to the surface, or to the photosphere, where it is released as heat, light, and other radiation.

definite yes. Three identifiable atmospheric layers ring the Sun: the photosphere, the chromosphere, and the corona. There is solar activity in all three.

What is the Sun's photosphere?

This could be called the Sun's surface. The sunlight we see comes from this layer of hot rising gases. The temperature in this layer gets lower as the gases move outward.

What is the Sun's chromosphere?

The chromosphere lies between the photosphere and the corona. The name means "sphere of color." This layer emits a pinkish glow that can only be seen during a total solar eclipse. The temperature in this layer also gets lower the farther out it goes.

What is the Sun's corona?

Seen only during a total solar eclipse, the corona has a brighter inner area called the K corona, and a duller outer area called the corona. Here temperatures rise the farther out the layer extends.

What is solar wind?

Not properly a layer of atmosphere, solar wind is a nonstop flow of particles from the Sun, launched by the high pressure in the corona. The particles race around at speeds of up to 621 miles (999.81 kilometers) per second.

The comet gets its name from the Greek word kometes, which means long hair.

What is a comet?

A comet is a strange space object that makes its way in and out of the orbits of planets. Some comets have definable orbits and some just seem to keep on flying, never to return. A comet has a head and tail. The head of a comet is largely composed of small particles of stony material cemented together by methane or ammonia frozen in ice particles. When the comet approaches the Sun, or another body with great heat or strong gravity, the head may break into pieces, leaving behind a meteor cloud or a long, sweeping tail.

Do comets ever hit planets?

Yes. In 1994, Jupiter was struck by 21 fragments of a large comet named Shoemaker-Levy 9.

Halley's Comet

Edmund Halley, who lived from 1656 to 1742, was a scientist, astronomer, and a friend of Sir Isaac Newton. He proved Newton's hypothesis that some comets followed elongated orbital paths, passing Earth on a regular schedule. Halley studied the path of a comet he watched in 1682 and compared its orbit to comets reported in 1456, 1531, and 1607. The paths matched, and Halley worked out that this was, in fact, the same comet appearing every 75 or 76 years. The comet was named after Halley and returned, as he predicted, in 1759. The last time Halley's comet passed near Earth was in 1986. Unfortunately, so much publicity and hype accompanied its expected return that when it did appear, many observers were disappointed.

This meteoroid might be heading for Earth. Gravity pulls these objects—some tiny, some large—into our atmosphere. Some burn up in the atmosphere, while others are large enough to make it to Earth's surface.

You can visit Meteor Crater in Arizona to see for yourself where a 60,000-ton (60,000,000-kilogram) meteorite hit Earth 20,000 years ago.

Astronomers had been waiting and watching. They were rewarded by a spectacular show as the comet fragments slammed into Jupiter's surface. Tremendous columns of gas and debris rose above the crash sites. Thousands of people photographed this event, which will yield fascinating data for years to come.

What's the difference between a meteor, a meteorite, and a meteoroid?

All three are masses of stone and metal from outer space. Meteors burn up in Earth's atmosphere before hitting the ground. These can sometimes be seen as shooting stars in the night sky. Meteorites make it through the atmosphere and make contact with Earth. Meteoroid is the term used for a meteor or meteorite before it reaches Earth's atmosphere.

What is an asteroid?

An asteroid is a meteoroid specifically orbiting the Sun between Jupiter and Mars. Asteroids are bigger than meteoroids. They measure up to 500 miles (805 kilometers) in diameter. Some observers believe asteroids may be the remains of a planet that disintegrated. Others think the fragments may have been leftover after the planets formed more than 4.6 billion years ago.

What is a meteor shower?

At various times of the year, Earth's orbit takes us through swarms of particles. The pull of Earth's gravity forces these particles to streak through the atmosphere, creating a display of shooting stars, as they are sometimes called. Whizzing downward, the meteors become visible at about 70 miles (112.7 kilometers) away. This usually happens at the same point in the sky every year, so the showers are given the name of the nearest star constellation. Around August 12, for instance, the Perseids appear to come from the constellation Perseus. Around November 17, the Leonids seem to spring from Leo. The meteors only seem to come from these constellations, however. Streaking meteors can be seen in almost any part of the sky.

What is a light-year?

Light-years are a measurement of distance in space. The concept was created to avoid having to use so many numbers to describe vast distance in miles. Over the distances we can see on Earth, light seems to travel instantly. It takes just over an eighth of a second for light to travel all the way around the world. In one second, light can travel 186,300 miles (299,943 kilometers). In one year, light will travel 5.88 trillion miles (9.4668 trillion kilometers): the distance of one light-year.

Meteorites

Meteorites have a long history on Earth. It has been suggested that the sacred Muslim Kaaba stone in Mecca is a large meteorite, and that in one temple dedicated to the Roman goddess Diana, a meteorite was worshiped. In the epic poem the *Iliad*, an iron meteorite is a trophy for the winner of a hero's funeral games.

Ancient civilizations, such as those of the Sumerians and the Hittites, used meteoric stone for weapons and tools. Since meteorites often contain iron and nickel, they made stronger, more durable instruments than earthen rock. Meteorites were treasured as fire from heaven or gifts of the gods.

The largest meteorite to have been discovered is in southwest Africa. The Hoba is a mass of iron weighing 66 tons (66,000 kilograms) and measuring about 9 feet (2.8 meters) across. Many samples of meteorites are displayed in museums worldwide. The 34-ton (31-metric-ton) meteorite Ahnighito fell in Greenland some 10,000 years ago and, before being sold to New York's American Museum of Natural History in 1897, supplied Greenlanders with material for knives and harpoon tips.

nen did life begin? ◆ How did life begin? ◆ What i
:ell? ◆ How did the first prokaryotic cells live?
ow did the first **THE** evolve? ◆ What made i
ssible for organism **THE** cmplex than cells t
pear? When did the first animal life appear?
hat i **BEGINNING** ozoan
ove around? ◆ What kind of life came afte
otozoans? ◆ What did he first recognizable lif
ok like? ◆ M **OF LIFE** d important
What are trilobites? ◆ When did vertebrate
·st appear? ◆ Why is an internal skeleto

When did life begin?

Evidence of the earliest life has been found in fossils dating back about 3.5 billion years, in the Precambrian era. The fossils are of microscopic plantlike single cells called blue-green algae, similar to bacteria today. Life, as we know it, did not exist before there was water, so sometime between 4.2 billion years ago (when scientists estimate water began to form on Earth) and 3.5 billion years ago, life began.

What is a geological age?

To help organize the study of prehistory, scientists have established a time line to break up vast amounts of time into smaller units. In the same way that we talk about Classical Rome, the Colonial Era, or the Industrial Revolution in history, we can speak of the Proterozoic eon, Paleozoic era, or the Jurassic period in prehistory.

Geological ages are based on Earth's stages of development. Time is broken down rather like a postal address into epochs, periods, eras, and eons:

Dinosaurs	(Life form)	Addressee
Early Jurassic	(Epoch/Period)	Street Address
Mesozoic	(Era)	City, State
Phanerozoic	(Eon)	Country
188 million years ago	(Date)	Zip Code

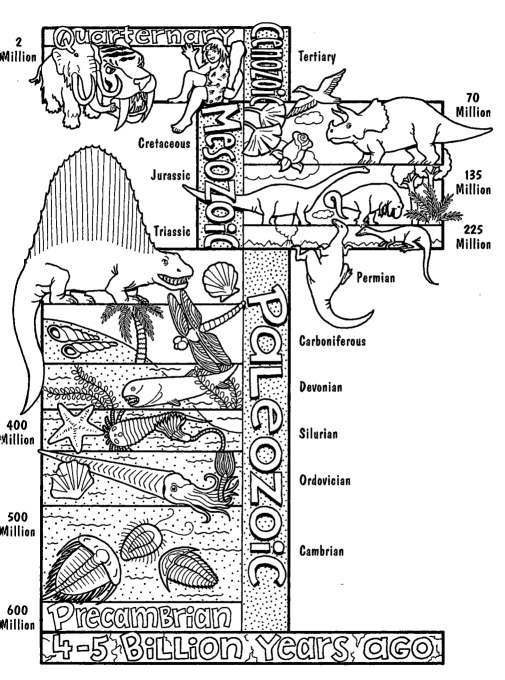

2 Million

Quarternary

Tertiary

70 Million

Cretaceous

135 Million

Jurassic

Triassic

225 Million

Permian

Carboniferous

Devonian

400 Million

Silurian

Ordovician

500 Million

Cambrian

600 Million

Precambrian

4-5 Billion Years ago

Cenozoic

Mesozoic

Paleozoic

Scientists use the geologic timetable to assign dates to events in Earth's history. The numbers above represent how long ago the corresponding period and era occurred.

Very Old Bacteria

One of the most remarkable opportunities to study prehistoric life surfaced in Elk Lake, Minnesota, in 1983. Frozen cells of 7,500-year-old bacteria were found embedded in the lake's mud. They were taken to a genetics lab in Denver, Colorado, where they were carefully warmed to air temperature. Sure enough, the cells began to multiply! How did they survive all those years? Researchers claimed that such simple cells had the ability to lower their metabolism (the rate of consuming and releasing energy) until the environment was better suited for their survival.

Another way of putting it is to say certain dinosaurs lived in the Early Jurassic period of the Mesozoic era in the Phanerozoic eon, about 188 million years ago.

How did life begin?

Nobody can answer this question completely. Taking into account everything we know about the physical makeup of the universe, life had to have come from the same raw ingredients as everything else: elements (such as nitrogen, hydrogen, oxygen, and carbon). One theory holds that ocean molecules containing carbon clustered together and developed the ability to make copies of themselves, or reproduce. Reproduction was the first sign of life.

What is a cell?

The simplest cells are not much more than microscopic pools of DNA (deoxyribonucleic acid) and enzymes wrapped in a thin shell called a membrane. A cell's DNA is a sort of code that programs the cell to operate—like software. Combinations of proteins form enzymes that carry out functions such as metabolism, the production and release of energy, through chemical reactions. The membrane simply holds the DNA and enzymes together in a single unit. These cells are called *prokaryotes.*

How did the first prokaryotic cells live?

Prokaryotes, the first single cells, basically did nothing more than eat and reproduce. A prokaryote ate by allowing the passage of **nutrients**, substances used for food, from the water through its membrane wall. It released byproducts back through the membrane. It reproduced by a method called **mitosis.** In mitosis, the DNA splits apart and the cell membrane folds in on the middle of the cell, cutting the one cell into two cells with identical DNA codes.

How did the first cells evolve?

How the identical single cells evolved into more complex cells is as little understood as how life initially began. We don't really know. What we do know, however, is that the prokaryotic cells developed nuclei. Nuclei, the plural of **nucleus**, are enclosed centers of operation, containing the DNA and enzymes that dictate the processes of life. Separating the essential information that runs the program of life provided physical protection for the all-important chemically coded programs. It also allowed for the development of specialized functions.

How did organisms more complex than cells appear?

Around 2.8 billion years ago, cells began to rely on sunlight for growth. In the process called **photosynthesis**, the cells used sunlight to change water into the simple sugars they needed for energy. Photosynthesis was probably the most important step in the **evolution** of life, or the process of changing and developing over time. This is because the energy source—the Sun—is almost unlimited.

When did the first animal life appear?

The first animals, called *protozoans*, appeared in the Proterozoic eon, a geological age that occurred from 2,500 to 570 million years ago. They were remarkably similar to the early plants. They were also single-celled, but the great advantage they had over plants was that they had **locomotion**: They could move around. Plants were **stationary**: They could not move around by themselves.

How did protozoans move around?

Some protozoans had a tail, called a **flagellum**, which propelled the cell by thrashing. Others had many hairlike filaments called **cilia**, which beat rhythmically, moving the cells through the water.

What kind of life came after protozoans?

Metazoans were the next stage of animal life. Though still very simple, metazoans were multicelled creatures rather than single cells. They developed systems of respiration, circulation, waste elimination, and sexual reproduction. Metazoans began to rely more and more on oxygen, which was becoming more plentiful in both the water and the air as a by-product of photosynthesis. Metazoans also began to feed on plants and each other.

What did the first recognizable life look like?

Invertebrates—creatures without internal skeletons or spines—were the earliest animals to evolve. They existed in the Proterozoic era, but it wasn't until the next era, the Paleozoic (570 million to 245 million years ago) that more familiar life forms proliferated. The first stretch of time in the Paleozoic era is called the Cambrian period. Sponges, coral, jellyfish, snails, clams, squids, worms, leeches, insects, spiders, lobsters, shrimp, sand dollars, and starfish have all been around since then.

Without internal skeletons, all of these creatures depended on the water around them or external skeletal structures, such as shells, for support.

Why is the Cambrian period important?

During the time before the Cambrian period (known as the Precambrian), evolutionary and geologic development was very slow. It took millions and billions of years for any changes to happen. With the Cambrian period, however, life forms evolved at a relatively rapid rate and have not stopped since.

Imagine, between 4.2 and 3.5 billion years ago, life originated on Earth. It took more than 3 billion years to get from these earliest life forms to those of the Cambrian period, but only 0.5 billion years to get from Cambrian life forms—such as trilobites—to human beings.

Trilobite fossils are abundant in rocks from the Cambrian period. This is part-ly because there were so many of them and because they had hard shells.

What are trilobites?

These early invertebrates were **crustaceans**, or sea creatures with hard shells. Trilobites were abundant in the Cambrian period. Most were no bigger than 4 inches (10 centimeters) long, although fossils found near Boston, Massachusetts, of one species of trilobite measure 18 inch-es (45 centimeters) long. All trilobites had bodies made up of three sections.

You can buy trilobite fossils in almost every fossil, rock, and nature store today.

When did vertebrates first appear?

The first **vertebrates**, or animals with internal skele-tons, developed in the water about 500 million years ago. Probably one of the earliest life forms with an internal skeleton most closely resembled echinoderms, which include starfish and sea urchins. Later, through many evo-lutionary changes, they grew fins and tails and evolved into fish.

Why is an internal skeleton important?

A skeleton inside the body provides support during growth, which allows vertebrates to grow larger than invertebrates. It also gives them a greater freedom of movement because internal skeletons are lighter than external ones. You can compare an internal skeleton to the frame of a kite. The kite's framework does not need to be large or heavy to give a big kite strength. On the other

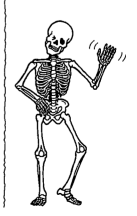

Evolution

Evolution is the process of change that enables life to adapt to its surroundings. When animals and some plants reproduce, each parent contributes half of the offspring's genetic information. The genes that are passed on to offspring are similar to, but never exactly the same as, the parent genes. While we are alive, our bodies can adapt to certain elements in our environment. For instance, an immunity to a disease can be developed and possibly passed on genetically to our offspring. The offspring would not have to develop that immunity, they would inherit it. In this way, the variety of possible life grows, from single cells to dinosaurs and humans.

hand, if the support were outside, like a shell, the kite would be so heavy that it would never get off the ground.

What were the first fish like?

Fossils of fish from the Ordovician period (500 million to 435 million years ago) can be found all over the world. They were primarily small fish, no bigger than a minnow, with plates that protected their heads, thin scales, and no jaws or teeth. These primitive fish probably lived near the bottom of shallow sea waters, living off food particles found in the mud. They had slits—not gills—on both sides of their throats, and their spines were more like flexible cartilage than bones. (Cartilage is rubbery bonelike material.)

The coelacanth is one type of fish that may be an ancestor of land animals. Scientists thought coelacanths were extinct until one was caught in 1938.

Were any of the earliest fish like the fish we know today?

In 1938, a large, ugly fish—the likes of which no scientist had ever seen—was found near the island of Madagascar. For fins it had fleshy stumps on which it could actually walk. It had a powerful jaw and square teeth. But the most astounding discovery was that this fish was a coelacanth.

The coelacanth first lived in the Devonian period. This contemporary descendant was almost identical to its ancestor, not changing significantly in 345 million years! Before 1938, biologists had believed that the coelacanth became extinct like the dinosaurs.

How did fish evolve?

The predator-prey relationship, in which some animals (predators) eat other animals (prey)—began when multicelled animals appeared. Jaws and teeth eventually became essential developments for survival in the ocean. The heavy protective plates of the early fish gave way to lighter scales. This change, along with the evolution of fins, allowed fish to swim in the water rather than inch along the bottom of the sea. These developments made it easier for them to search for food and to escape becoming food for another fish.

Did fish really crawl out onto land?

The famous coelacanth's stumpy fins are believed to have evolved so that it could walk on land. This fish also developed the ability to gulp air and absorb it through its **gullet**, or throat. So the coelacanth could not only walk on land, it could breathe. Another fish that developed the ability to gulp air is the lungfish. A few types of lungfish still exist in Africa, Australia, and South America.

Fossils show that other fishes began to find homes in shallower waters and wet mud along the shores. Over a period of 50 million years, their offspring became comfortable on the damp land above the waterline. These were the earliest **tetrapods**, or four-legged animals.

When did plants begin to grow on land?

The first plants to begin growing on land were bacteria, or microscopic plants, in the Ordovician period (505 to 438 million years ago). Lichens, mosses, and liverworts followed the bacteria onto land. Before the Ordovician period ended, a varied plant population—including ferns and trees—extended all over Earth's land masses.

What were the first plants like?

The bacteria that first grew on land evolved to survive in the harsh environment of ultraviolet sun rays, desert conditions, and lack of oxygen. The bacteria churned the rock into sediment, without which future land plants probably would not have been able to take root. It also provided plants with nutrients in the form of minerals on which to survive.

During the Silurian period, which followed the Ordovician period, forests of fernlike trees evolved. By the end of the Devonian period, some 360 million years ago, a varied plant population extended all over Earth's land masses.

How did trees develop?

The first trees were actually ferns, some reaching heights of 100 feet (30 meters). During the Devonian period, about 408 to 360 million years ago, ferns spread across the land. During the succeeding Carboniferous period (360 to 286 million years ago) huge forests were established, containing a variety of plants and trees.

Plants evolved just as animals evolved, and for the same reason—to enhance their chances for survival. Some adapted to living in the shade of trees. Some grew completely along the swampy forest floor or climbed up the trunks of trees to reach the sun.

Trees with highly developed patterns of foliage evolved. Tree branches figuratively fought for the most exposure to sunlight, the plant life's source of energy. The shape, number, and pattern of leaves evolved in order to catch the most sunlight possible. In the same way, root structures developed in competition for soil nutrients and moisture.

Dead and decaying plant life returned nutrients to the soil in the dense forests. Layers of this rotting material, called peat, were so plentiful that much of it was buried before fully breaking down into soil. Mud encased the peat and, over time, more peat and more mud compressed—as a result of gravity, lack of oxygen, and chemistry—into coal. The age of great forests was in the Carboniferous period, which means the "coal-bearing" period.

What other animals, besides tetrapods, found their way onto land?

Long before **tetrapods**, primitive invertebrates, including insects, populated the land. Invertebrate creatures on about one hundred legs and ancestors of spiders came ashore during the Silurian period (about 435 million years ago).

Imagine Earth inhabited by nothing but centipedes and spiders!

Did dinosaurs evolve from tetrapods?

Long ago in geological history, *all* vertebrates, including dinosaurs, evolved from the first tetrapods. Most directly, dinosaurs evolved from crocodilelike animals, a group of reptiles called crocodilians. Crocodile fossils from the Triassic period (250 million years ago) can be found all over the world.

When did dinosaurs appear?

Fossil records show that dinosaurs developed during the Triassic period of the Mesozoic era (250 to 65 million years ago).

Just before the Triassic period, there was a mass **extinction**, or dying out, of animal life, probably as a result of severe environmental changes. Many species became extinct. The dinosaurs initially had little competition.

How did the dinosaurs evolve?

Dinosaurs evolved from a reptile called a thecodont, which seems to have been the ancestor of birds as well. Thecodonts were medium-size predators that lived in the Permian and Triassic periods on land that was thawing after a recent **ice age**, a time of cold temperatures and widespread **glaciers**, or layers of ice.

The carnivorous *Tyrannosaurus rex* was huge, the largest meat-eating animal known. *Tyrannosaurus* bones were first discovered in 1902 in Montana.

Dinosaurs diversified in many different directions. *Camptosaurus* was a 25-foot **herbivore** (plant-eater), but many other early dinosaurs were much smaller—even as small as a chicken. Some were **carnivorous** (meat-eating) predators. A number of early dinosaurs began walking on two legs rather than four, thus becoming the earliest **bipedal** creatures.

Within 10 million years, dinosaurs of all varieties reigned over Earth.

How can we know about the habits of dinosaurs when all we have are fossils?

It is amazing how much can be deciphered from a fossil. For instance, scientists can often tell what dinosaurs ate by studying their fossil remains. If a fossil of a dinosaur shows that it had sharp teeth and claws, scientists can figure that it was a meat-eating dinosaur. Meat-eating dinosaurs were bipedal, which allowed them to run swiftly after prey. If a fossil seems to show that the living creature walked on two legs, that might also indicate that it ate other animals. Plant-eaters had teeth suitable for grinding vegetation. Many were quadrupeds, meaning they walked on four legs. Fossils with these characteristics are of plant-eating dinosaurs.

The depth of fossilized footprints can be used to calculate the weight of dinosaurs. Some of the most impressive fossils are those of dinosaur tracks. Footprints also confirm that many dinosaurs traveled in groups, with younger dinosaurs in the middle of the herd where they would be protected. These were herbivorous dinosaurs, their social structure resembling herd animals (such as water buffalo) of today.

Why did the dinosaurs disappear?

No one knows the answer for sure. Dinosaurs of many different types—from small to huge, meat-eating and herbivorous—roamed the entire Earth. They had existed for 150 million years.

Scientists debate many different theories about why the dinosaurs disappeared, and they seem to agree on only one thing: Something big happened at the end of the Cretaceous period (about 65 million years ago) that altered the environment so that it no longer supported dinosaurs—and many other living creatures.

Does extinction still happen?

Yes. Changes in weather, occurrence of disease, environmental disasters (natural or caused by humans), and competition can all cause the extinction of life. Actually, there is evidence that throughout time, more species have

Scientists sometimes call *Triceratops* "the last of the dinosaurs" because its fossil remains are found in the most recent rocks containing dinosaur fossils.

become extinct than have survived. There is no instance of a complete extinction of life on the planet. Always, some lineages have survived. For example, when dinosaurs became extinct around the end of the Cretaceous period, mammals survived.

What animals have become extinct?

The list—from the beginning of life to the present day—is far too great to give here. The dodo bird's story is interesting as an example because it happened recently—recently that is, in geologic time.

In the sixteenth century, sailors populated the island of Mauritius in the Indian Ocean. So did dodo birds. They were large, seemingly stupid birds that could not fly. Their extinction came about through competition among different species. Sailors killed dodos easily for food, while the pigs and rats that came to the island with the sailors ate dodo eggs. Within one hundred years, dodos no longer existed.

Are species still in danger of becoming extinct?

The blue whale has become so rare that it is unlikely that the few individuals left will be able to meet and reproduce.

According to figures gathered by the United Nations, there are more than 4,000 plants and 5,000 animals that may not survive into the twenty-first century. The list covers lizards and insects that live in the tops of rain-forest trees, which are being cut down at a great rate. The elm tree, once abundant in the United States, has been decimated by Dutch elm disease.

When did mammals first appear on Earth?

Mammals actually originated at about the same time that dinosaurs did. They lived together for about 150 million years before dinosaurs died out. During that time, mammals did not get bigger and were most likely nocturnal. But once the dinosaurs were out of the way, mammals flourished.

Why did the mammals survive?

Scientists don't know for certain why some animals survived the time of great extinction at the end of the Cretaceous period. Whatever the cause, it was a time of rapid change in the environment. It is possible that mammals could adapt to the new environment quickly enough to survive. At this time, mammals were small **nocturnal** (nighttime) creatures. Their size meant that they didn't need a lot of food for survival. The fact that they came out at night and remained in underground burrows during the day protected them from the Sun's ultraviolet rays. These two factors might have kept them from dying out with the dinosaurs.

What distinguishes mammals from other animal species?

Scientists use two identifying characteristics to say: "This is a mammal." The two mammalian **traits** are that females produce milk to nurse their young, and that mammals have hair or fur on their bodies. Many traits are shared with other species, and not all mammmmals have the same traits, except for these two. That's how whales and humans can be of the same species.

How did mammals evolve?

After the mass extinction of dinosaurs and other life forms, mammal evolution did not happen gradually, but in fits and starts. About 54 million years ago, during the Tertiary period (approximately 65 million to 3 million years ago), the variety of mammals evolved rapidly. Ancestors of porpoises, dolphins, and whales populated the oceans. Early hoofed mammals—ancestors of horses, pigs, and sheep—roamed on land.

When did humans appear?

This is not an easy question to answer. Debates rage over which fossils can be called truly *hominoid* (human-like), or **hominid** (human).

The development of human characteristics took place over millions of years. The earliest **primate** (an order of mammals that includes humans, apes, and monkeys), no bigger than a rat, appeared 60 million years ago. About 10 million years ago, the *Ramapithecus* showed remarkable hominoid attributes. But there is no further evidence until 6 million years later. The first generally accepted hominoid is called *Australopithecus,* and some believe they are actually the most primitive of the human lineage.

Homo habilis, dating back at least 2 million years in modern-day Africa, is undisputedly human. Less than a half-million years later, *Homo erectus* lived in Africa as well as in Asia and Europe. A fossil skull fragment discovered in England is the oldest known example of modern-day humans: a 300,000-year-old *Homo sapien.*

Lucy

Lucy is one of the oldest and most important fossil skeletons ever discovered. The archaeologists took her name from the Beatles' song "Lucy in the Sky with Diamonds," which, in 1974, played over and over in their campsite. Her scientific name is *Australopithecus afarensis.* A team of researchers led by Dr. Donald C. Johansen uncovered 40 percent of her skeleton, quite a complete finding compared to other hominoids of her age. She is about 3.4 million years old.

One day, Dr. Johansen noticed an arm bone sticking out of the ground in the Ethiopian valley where the archaeologists were digging. After 3 weeks of meticulous sand and sediment sifting, Lucy appeared. The fact that her jaw showed the presence of wisdom teeth led experts to estimate that she was about 20 years old when she died. Using Lucy's thigh bone as a measure, they determined her height to be about 3½ feet (105 centimeters). As with other *Australopithecus,* Lucy walked upright and had a relatively small brain.

The following year, 1975, archaeologists uncovered the fragments of bones from some of Lucy's kin, approximately thirteen individuals, including men, women, and children. The placement of the bones suggested that all of them died together—but how? The scientists examined the ground in which the bones were found and speculated that the bones were carried a distance by a flood. Because the bones lay together more or less in a heap and were covered in the same silt, it is probable that they were suddenly deposited at a point where the rushing floodwater slowed quickly upon reaching a wide open area. This would allow the bones to sink to the bottom all together. Then the sediment carried by the floodwaters would have settled over them, providing a wonderful environment for immediate burial and subsequent fossilization.

Did the different hominid species ever live together?

Just because scientists give dates to these findings, don't be fooled into thinking the evolution of humans is completely understood. Who knows what may still lie buried in Earth's crust and from when? Also, the appearance of a new species doesn't mean that the previous one had already died out. It is believed, for example, that *Homo habilis* and *Homo erectus* lived side-by-side each other, along with *Australopithecus.*

Human Speech

By studying fossils, scientists have determined that, indeed, prehistoric people probably talked to each other in some form of language. We can't say when, exactly, language developed, but 2-million-year-old fossils of human skulls show the two specific bulges where the brain now controls speech. The bulges appear in the left side of the brain. One controls the physical movements for speech and the other is necessary for understanding speech. Specimens of *Homo erectus, Homo habilis,* and *Homo sapiens* all show these bulges.

Australopithecus afarensis is about 3 million years old, and is the scientific name for the fossil scientists call Lucy.

Homo habilis means "handy man." *Homo habilis* used simple stone tools.

Homo erectus, a more advanced hominid than *Homo habilis,* appeared 1.5 million years ago.

you dug a hole to the center of Earth, wha
uld you find? What is Earth's crust made of

EARTH

What is Ear lithosphere What is Earth'
thenosphere? How far is it to the center o
rth? How can we determine the makeup an

INSIDE AND

nper ur sa t we n t it o
en see it? Do all scientists agree on what'
ide Earth? ◆ Wh t the core made of rock?

OUT

w hot is Earth' co ? s anything happe
ide Earth? ◆ Wha is rock made of? ◆ What ar
eous rocks? ◆ How are sedimentary rock

If you dug a hole to the center of Earth, what would you find?

Earth has several layers. We live on the crust: the outer, rigid layer called the lithosphere, which includes both the continents and the ocean basins. Beneath the crust lies a very hot, partly molten section known as the mantle. The uppermost section of the mantle is called the asthenosphere, and is plastic, or flexible. It is about 100 miles (160 kilometers) thick and is composed of molten rock, or magma. Below that, the rock is solid again because the pressure consolidates molten rock and liquids into hard rock and other solids.

Deep within Earth lies the core, which has two distinct layers. The outer core is liquid and contains iron, nickel, and various other metals. The inner core is a solid ball of iron and nickel 1,500 miles (2,400 kilometers) in diameter.

What is Earth's crust made of?

Earth's crust contains an abundance of chemicals, elements, minerals, and rocks. Though there was a time when oxygen was nonexistent, it is now the most common element. It makes up about 20 percent of the air in its gaseous form, but is also found in combination with other materials in the crust. Nearly 50 percent of Earth's

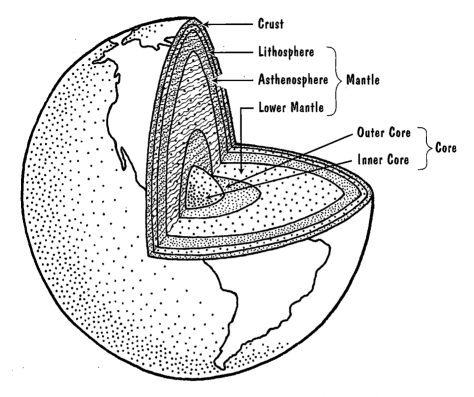

Earth is made up of several layers around a very dense, solid core. Scientists learn about the interior of Earth by studying vibrations from earthquakes.

crust is made up of combinations of oxygen with other substances.

Sand and rock is mostly silicon and oxygen, and there is plenty of sand and rock around. These make up about 28 percent of the crust. Most of the rock on Earth is granite, molten rock that has cooled slowly.

Aluminum, found in almost all natural clay in the world, makes up a little less than 9 percent of the crust. More than 4 percent of the crust is iron and 3.5 percent is calcium. The remaining 5.5 percent of the crust comes from another ten elements and traces of many others.

What is Earth's lithosphere?

The lithosphere, or "rocky globe," is the scientific name for the land and ocean floor, the tectonic plates, and the rocky base on which they rest. Essentially, the lithosphere comprises the crust of Earth.

What is Earth's asthenosphere?

This layer lies just below the lithosphere. It is the upper layer of the mantle and is molten rock. The asthenosphere is the section that is constantly, though relatively slowly, flowing. As it moves, the lithosphere moves with it.

How far is it to the center of Earth?

We know Earth's diameter is approximately 7,900 miles (12,640 kilometers). Half of that is Earth's radius, the distance to the center. The crust runs approximately 55 miles (88 kilometers) deep. The mantle is about 1,800 miles (2,880 kilometers) deep; the outer core, approximately 1,400 miles (2,240 kilometers); and the inner core about 750 miles (1,200 kilometers). Added together, that makes the distance to the center of Earth about 3,900 miles (6,240 kilometers). That's just short of our 7,900-mile (12,640-kilometer) diameter (twice the radius) but, remember, these are approximations.

How hot is Earth's core?

Two factors determine the heat at the center of Earth: pressure and radioactive energy (the energy released by changes in atomic levels). These amount to an impressive temperature, at least 5,000° Fahrenheit (2,760° Celsius). Some estimates place the temperature as high as 7,000° (3,870° Celsius).

Does anything happen inside Earth?

Plenty. Nothing is static in the universe; things are happening everywhere.

For starters, the many chemicals in molten rock interact with each other, under heat and pressure, to form new substances. Some of these substances are minerals, crystals, precious metals—such as gold and silver—and gems—such as diamonds, rubies, and emeralds.

What is rock made of?

Rocks are combinations of minerals, which are often in crystal form. Diamonds are rocks just as stones on the seashore are rocks. Most rocks contain different combinations of about twenty of the same minerals, including silicon, calcium, iron, and magnesium. Rocks fall into three main classifications according to how they are formed: igneous, sedimentary, and metamorphic.

What are igneous rocks?

Igneous rock results from the cooling and combining of molten minerals. The molten material is called **magma** when it lies beneath Earth's surface and **lava** when it reaches the surface. The type of igneous rocks formed depends not only on which minerals are present, but how quickly the lava cools and solidifies. Lava that cools quickly, usually when it suddenly comes into contact with air or water hundreds of degrees lower than the lava's temperature, creates glass. **Obsidian**, or volcanic glass, is formed this way. If the lava cools slowly, over years, the minerals combine differently, creating solid masses of rock.

How are sedimentary rocks formed?

Sedimentary rock contains fragments of other rocks that have been broken down into small particles. These particles are carried by glaciers, rivers, the wind, landslides, wave action, and many other modes of transportation. Fossilized plant and animal matter are commonly found in sedimentary rock.

Element Chart

Most Common Elements Found in the Universe

	Name	Symbol
1.	Hydrogen	H
2.	Helium	He
3.	Oxygen	O
4.	Carbon	C
5.	Phosphorous	P
6.	Neon	Ne
7.	Nitrogen	N
8.	Magnesium	Mg
9.	Silicon	Si
10.	Iron	Fe
11.	Sulfur	S
12.	Argon	Ar
13.	Aluminum	Al
14.	Calcium	Ca
15.	Sodium	Na
16.	Chromium	Cr
17.	Manganese	Mn
18.	Chlorine	Cl
19.	Potassium	K
20.	Titanium	Ti

Lithification is the process by which these particles become one solid rock, or sedimentary rock. It can occur by three separate processes: cementation, compaction, and desiccation. Cementation occurs when binding minerals (like clay) or other substances form between the particles of sediment. While the rock is being cemented, more particles are transported on top of it. As the particles build up—and are also cemented—the weight and pressure from above causes the lower rock to reduce in volume, much like trash in a trash compactor. Compaction causes desiccation, which is the squeezing out of water.

The process of lithification creates different layers of sediment in the rock, depending on what sediment is currently being deposited. In this way, sedimentary rock provides a time line for Earth's history. The different layers, or **strata**, can show what was occurring on Earth's surface, and for how long, and what life forms were active.

What are metamorphic rocks?

Metamorphic rocks are rocks that have changed their structure and chemical composition. Heat, pressure, and chemical activity can each cause the changes.

When a rock comes into contact with extreme heat, the atoms within expand and loosen or break their bonds with other atoms. The loose atoms then circulate within the rock, forming new minerals. The rock is literally transformed into another kind of rock.

Pressure ultimately has the same effect on rock, but through compression rather than expansion. Pressure squeezes the rock until the atoms break apart and make new, more compact, bonds, which makes a harder, denser new rock.

The various minerals in a rock react differently to chemicals, forming new atomic structures to become other minerals. Chemicals that cause these changes can be found deep within Earth and in cooling magma. The presence of water can cause transformation as well, since certain minerals alter their structure when they come into contact with water.

A wonderful result of rock metamorphosis, or change, is marble. Under heat and pressure limestone commonly forms marble, without which many of the world's sculpture treasures would not exist.

How can you tell older from younger layers of rock?

Older rock tends to lie underneath younger rock. As a general rule, this works, but there are many factors to take into consideration.

Earth's surface constantly moves and shifts. Sometimes, older rock is folded on top of younger rock, or catapulted from a volcano, for instance. To take these events into account, the whole composition of a rock formation must be considered. Superposition says that the uppermost layer of rock is younger than what is below it. However, if you find a layered rock that is folded over other rock (a consequence of an earthquake, for instance), to figure out the relative ages of the layers, you must imagine unfolding the whole formation instead of just looking at one piece of it.

Perhaps a shaft of magma shot upward from the mantle, but didn't break through the surface. Imagine three layers: limestone, shale, and sandstone. Suddenly a mile down the road, the layers become limestone, shale, granite, and sandstone. The problem to solve is how the granite got there. It is likely that at some point, a channel of magma tried to escape to the surface, but was stopped and metamorphosed into granite. The granite would still be younger than the rock it had cut through, even though it appeared third from the top.

How do we tell the actual age of rock?

Radiocarbon dating, developed in the 1940s, is based on the presence of a variant form—isotope—of the element carbon that exists in rocks. Many elements have a variety of atomic isotopes. For instance, most carbon atoms have a mass of 12 units, but the carbon atoms used in radiocarbon dating have a mass of 14 units. This isotope is known as carbon-14.

Isotopes are measured by the rate of their radioactive decay, which begins as soon as the rock is formed. The isotopes used in dating decompose very slowly, over millions of years, at a predictable rate called a half-life. As they break down, they leave behind what is known as the decay product. For instance, when carbon-14 decays, nitrogen-14 takes its place. When one half-life is over, the sample of rock has 50 percent carbon-14 and 50 percent nitrogen-14. Each successive half-life reduces the remaining amount of the isotope by 50 percent, so after the second half-life, the sample shows 25 percent carbon-14 and 75 percent nitrogen-14.

The half-life of carbon-14 is 5,700 years. Therefore, if a sample has 50 percent carbon-14 and 50 percent nitrogen-14, we know it is 5,700 years old. A measurement of 25 percent carbon-14 and 75 percent nitrogen-14 means the rock is 11,400 years old. Carbon dating is used for rocks between 100 and 70,000 years old. For older rocks, isotopes with longer half-lives are necessary. Potassium-40 has a half-life of 1.3 billion years and is used for dating rocks older than 70,000 years.

Mohs' Hardness Scale

Mohs' hardness scale rates minerals from the softest (1) to the hardest (10). The softer a mineral, the easier it is to scratch it. For comparison: a fingernail rates 2.5; human teeth, 5; and glass, 6.

1	Talc
2	Gypsum
3	Calcite
4	Fluorite
5	Apatite
6	Orthoclase
7	Quartz
8	Topaz
9	Corundum
10	Diamond

What is soil made of?

Soil is generally made up of many different minerals, elements, and organic matter. The dirt of different areas has specific components—such as aluminum, iron, quartz, sand, acid, or salt—which is why some plants grow better in some places than in others.

What are minerals?

A mineral is a unique composition of elements. For instance, silicon and dioxide interact chemically to form quartz. The most common mineral, feldspar, which makes up about half of Earth's crust, is aluminum plus sodium, calcium, or potassium.

Minerals will separate from cooling magma and make their way through veins into surrounding rock, called ore. Miners search for these veins to find the minerals they contain. Some veins contain single-element minerals such as copper.

What are crystals?

Crystals are geometric mineral growths containing mostly oxygen. Minerals develop unique crystals, which help to identify the exact mineral. Quartz crystals, for example, are the crystals that develop from the mineral quartz (silicon and dioxide). Layers of atoms adhere to a seed crystal, and grow in geometric configurations, such as cubes or tetrahedrons (shapes with four planes, or faces).

How are minerals identified?

Go into any rock shop and you will see the variety of beautiful crystals in all shapes, sizes, colors, and brilliance. These factors are exactly what help geologists identify the minerals from which the crystals have grown. Geometric shape, color, luster, hardness, density, transparency, fluorescence—even taste and smell—are qualities that identify a given mineral.

How are gold and silver formed?

Gold is an element, meaning that it is not formed, but exists as an atomic structure. It came into existence in Earth's greenstone belts—recrystallized lava and sediment—about 4 billion years ago. Large deposits are extracted through mining. Small bits of gold can be sifted out of gold-rich streams because gold is heavier than most sand and gravel.

One ounce of gold can be beaten into a thin sheet 100 square feet (9.3 square meters).

For more than 6,000 years, gold has been a symbol of status and wealth. It does not tarnish or corrode and it is very malleable, or flexible.

Silver is an element more common than gold. In the Nevada Comstock Lode, discovered in 1859, the silver ore formed a slab 400 feet (122 meters) thick and 3,000 feet (915 meters) deep.

How are gems created and extracted?

Gems result from the crystallization of minerals or elements when they contact oxygen underground. A wide variety exists: quartz gems, transparent gems, opaque gems, and, of course, diamonds.

Most commonly, gems are mined from the ground like minerals and metals. (Pearls, however, are harvested from oysters.) For thousands of years, humans have dug for precious materials. Sometimes, however, underground

Gold Discovery

Discoveries of gold in the American West during the mid-nineteenth century inspired thousands of prospectors. There were stories of gold simply lying on the ground, mountains of gold, and enough gold for all. The truth was quite different.

Finding gold has never been an easy task. Mining is dangerous and difficult and depends a lot on luck. Stumbling across gold out in the open is not common. If it were, and if there truly were enough gold for all, who would care? Part of gold's importance is that it is rare and difficult to attain.

Not so for one prospector— Richard Stoddard—at least for a while. Like so many others, Stoddard and his partner set off in 1849 for the Sierra Nevada, a mountain range in California. In their search, they came upon a lake—filled with gold nuggets, so Stoddard said.

Stoddard and his partner stuffed their pockets with all they could carry and went to gather supplies and enlist help for gathering their fortune. It took weeks to find the way back to civilization, and Stoddard's comrade died along the way. Stoddard himself was in bad shape when he finally reached Sacramento, but he was anxious to get back to his lake of gold. The image of a clear mountain lake with the sun shining off layers of nuggets was tantalizing. Backers financed a return trip to the lake with Stoddard. But Stoddard got lost in the mountains. He could not find his lake of gold. Finally, the financial backers gave him one last chance—24 more hours—to lead them to the gold, or they would hang him. That night, Stoddard disappeared. The region where he claimed the lake of gold to be is called Last Chance Valley to this day.

shifts cause lava and rock to force their way to the surface. The underground wealth has no choice but to go along for the ride.

What are quartz gems?

Quartz gems—crystallized minerals—are the most common semiprecious stones. The crystal quartz amethyst contains iron, which causes sunlight to refract shades of purple. The fiery flashes of fluorescent colors in opals, which form in hot water springs, probably result from the unique layering of mineral crystals in this uncommon environment.

What are transparent gems?

If light can get through a substance, it is considered transparent. Crystallized elements create rubies, emeralds, sapphires, and zircon, some of the more familiar precious transparent stones.

Zircons, often substituted for diamonds, can be made a rich blue by heating the stones in the absence of air.

Most transparent gems come from the elements aluminum, beryllium, or magnesium. Rubies and sapphires have virtually the same elemental base, but slight differences result in a spectrum of reds in rubies and violet, green, and yellow in emeralds.

What are opaque gems?

Stones—or anything else—that cannot be seen through are called opaque. Metallic ores and rock minerals create opaque crystals. Turquoise comes from copper and sometimes shows veins of clay or iron oxide, giving it a cracked look. Common opaque jade crystallizes from the mineral pyroxene, which in sunlight usually looks green, but may appear in pink, white, and yellow.

What is so special about diamonds?

Carbon subjected to intense pressure and heat far down in Earth's interior becomes compacted and incredibly hard; in this state it is called a diamond—the hardest known natural substance on Earth. Not only do diamonds possess great beauty, but also great utility. The sparkle and brilliance of diamonds come from the way the light refracts through this hardened element. And its hardness

makes it extremely useful in cutting virtually anything with great precision.

Where can diamonds be found?

Diamonds rarely appear in sufficient quantity to make mining practical or affordable. Until 1725, diamonds were mined almost solely in India. They were then discovered in enough quantity to be mined in Brazil. The largest deposits of diamonds have been found near Kimberley, South Africa. Most of the diamonds in the world are now mined in Africa, though half of them are used for industrial purposes rather than as jewels.

Diamonds are found in small amounts in many other places worldwide. In the United States, diamonds have

Kohinoor Diamond

You can see one of the most famous diamonds in history, the Kohinoor, almost any day in London, England. The first record of this fabulous diamond is in the year 1304 in India, where it belonged to a rajah. It was passed on to each ruler until the Persian invasion of 1739. But the conquering shah could not find the diamond for several months. It was hidden in the rajah's turban. When it was finally discovered, the legend tells that the shah exclaimed "Koh-i-noor!" which means "a mountain of light."

The shah was soon assassinated, and the Kohinoor went to his son. The diamond seemed ill-fated, however. The son was tortured to reveal its whereabouts. He didn't say, but the diamond was discovered and the son died. The Kohinoor passed from generation to generation, with many of its owners tortured to discover where the diamond was hidden. The head of one live man was boiled and other men were blinded to force them to tell.

In 1813, the diamond belonged to Ranjit Singh, an Indian ruler. When the British colonized India after his death, the jewel became the property of Queen Victoria. Victoria was not satisfied with the gem and had it recut, reducing it from its original weight of 186 carats (1 carat is equal to 200 milligrams) to 109 carats. She then wore it as a pin. When King George V ascended the throne in 1910, the Kohinoor was set in Queen Mary's crown. In 1957, it was reset in Queen Elizabeth II's crown. That crown and the Kohinoor can be viewed at the Tower of London for the cost of a ticket.

been found on the beaches of northern California, in the Appalachian Mountains, and in glacial deposits in Ohio, Michigan, and Wisconsin. The only actual diamond mine in the United States was in Arkansas. It yielded some 40,000 diamonds and is now a tourist attraction.

What is graphite?

Graphite is a layered form of carbon. The chemical bonding within the layers is as strong as in a diamond, but the bonding between layers is so weak, we use graphite in soft "lead" pencils rather than in engagement rings.

When did people start using minerals?

One of the most important early mineral finds was obsidian. Obsidian comes from the terrific heat beneath Earth's crust. It spews up in volcanoes as lava and hardens into volcanic glass. When shattered, obsidian separates into knife-edged flakes. These flakes can be as sharp as a razor.

Some of the earliest humans set and bound obsidian flakes into sticks of wood, making combination knife-saws. When treated with care and respect, these natural knives could be used for years.

Where does oil come from?

Oil is formed deep within Earth, underwater. Oil began its existence as microscopic sea vegetation. When the plants died and were covered by sediments, they were squeezed by the great force of pressure and became oil. Oil may come to Earth's surface on its own as a result of underground activity, or it can be extracted with drills and pumps, which is more common.

We call oil a fossil fuel because it comes from fossilized plant life and we use it for energy. Heaters, cars, and factories, among a huge number of other industrial-age inventions, depend on oil and other fossil fuels for energy.

What are fossils?

Remains, impressions, and outlines of plant and animal organisms—from single-celled vegetation to *Homo sapiens*—have been preserved, under certain conditions, in the rock record. These preserved materials, called fossils, give us an enormous amount of information about the prehistoric past.

What conditions are best for creating and preserving fossils?

The hard parts of an organism—such as the shell, bones, or teeth—are most often fossilized. These hard body parts are more likely than soft tissue to withstand destruction.

Second, the environment must be right to keep the object from decay. Rapid burial or submersion in water is

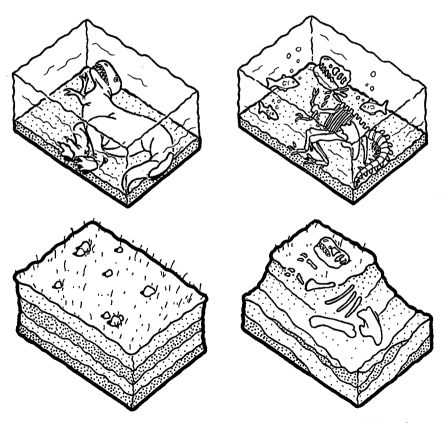

This series of drawings (starting on the upper left and moving clockwise) shows how some fossils form. The soft parts of the dinosaur's body decay, leaving the bones to be preserved in sediment. After millions of years, the rocks containing the dinosaur fossil are exposed on the surface.

necessary to encase the organism before bacteria, erosion, or predators get to it. Water environments are where most fossilization occurs, since sediment generally provides protection from the erosion and weathering that can destroy objects on land.

Are there different kinds of fossils?

The most informative fossils preserve the actual remains of an organism. For instance, the skeleton of a vertebrate may be fossilized intact. This occurs when minerals seep into the pores of the bone and petrify it. The bones are no longer composed of the same elements and minerals as they were when the animal was living. However, they still have a lot of information to provide.

Trace fossils are the preserved impressions of animals or plants, similar to the impression of your hand in clay or cement. The organism decomposes in water, but an imprint of it is rapidly filled by sediment, preserving it indefinitely. More information has been lost in this process, but a cast of the organism is left behind.

Carbon acts to preserve an impression of an organism, though usually one more delicate than a skeleton: a leaf or fragile animal. Over time, pressure from the fossil's rock eliminates liquid and gas, leaving behind carbon. The carbon leaves a shadow of the surface of the organism, sometimes in great detail.

Almost a whole world can be re-created from remains found in ice—even what the person ate the day he or she died, millions of years ago.

Another kind of fossil is a whole organism trapped in fossilized tree sap (amber). Insects and other small organisms such as lizards or spiders were sometimes trapped in tree sap that later hardened. The jewellike fossils reveal an actual organism millions of years old.

Ice is another preserver, if left undisturbed. Nearly intact human (as well as animal) remains have been discovered in ice.

Are footprints fossils?

Preserved footprints are trace fossils. Some prehistoric creatures are known today solely because they left their footprints behind. Footprints need a soft, moist, fine-grained surface—such as volcanic ash or mud—in order to be preserved. Impressions of claws, the shape of a

The footprint of a large mammal discovered in 1976 led to the surprising conclusion that humans were walking upright long before anyone had guessed.

heel, or direction of a toe can provide new insights into evolution.

What is the difference between Earth's continental crust and the oceanic crust?

The names give away their locations. The oceanic layer, underneath all of the oceans, is only 2.5 to 3 miles (4 to 5 kilometers) thick at its deepest and is very dense. The continental crust can be up to 40 miles (64 kilometers) thick. It is not as dense as the oceanic crust, so it is more buoyant, or capable of floating. The continental crust extends out into the oceans up to 200 miles (320 kilometers) before sloping off. This continental crust under water is known as the continental shelf.

How did the continental and oceanic crusts form?

At the beginning of Earth's history, there was no land or crust as we know it today. Earth's elements were still hot and in a molten state. As Earth cooled, pieces of a crust began to form at the top, much like the skin that forms on hot chocolate as it cools. This crust material became a different compound from its parent compound (the molten liquid) as it cooled. This happens because individual elements cool at different temperatures. The material that cooled first, the oceanic crust, is called basalt.

The continental crust is more complex. It is composed of many kinds of rock that came from uplifted basalt and basalt that remelted in the molten liquid after a collision with another piece of crust. This is similar to the top layer of hot chocolate that remelts if you stir it up. Early in Earth's history, the remelted basalt then came to the surface in volcanoes, forming different compounds that were lighter and more buoyant than the original basalt, forming proto-continents. This is why continents are not generally covered by water: They float on the molten liquid underneath.

Did proto-continents become the continents we know today?

Yes and no. *Proto* is a prefix meaning "the earliest form of," so you can tell from the word that proto-continents were the earliest form of continents. But a lot happened in between proto-continents and today's continents. Very little material making up our continents comes from those original land masses. Much of the continental crust is now composed of other kinds of rocks, like sedimentary rocks.

How did proto-continents lead to our continents?

As the proto-continents floated around, they sometimes collided and stuck together, a process called accretion. Early in Earth's history, all of the continents came together to form one giant continent. This occurred in the Proterozoic era, about 1,250 million years ago. At the time, there was only unicellular (one-celled) life on Earth. That continent broke up, but much later, in the Permian period (270 million years ago), a continent scientists call

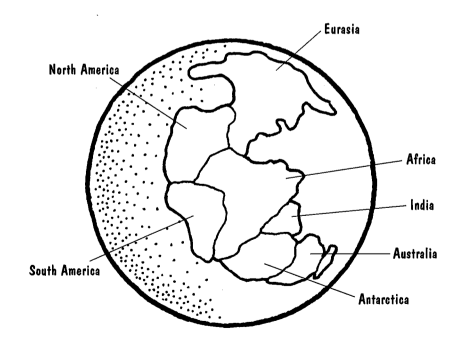

At one time all of the continents on Earth formed one land mass called Pangaea.

Pangaea is a Greek word meaning "all earth."

Pangaea formed. Life at this time consisted of invertebrates, fish, and amphibians. About 230 million years ago, Pangaea split into two large continents: Laurasia, which included North America, Greenland, and Eurasia; and Gondwanaland, which included South America, Africa, Australia, and Antarctica. This split happened just before the age of the dinosaurs. About 80 million years ago, at the end of the Cretaceous period, the land masses began to split up to resemble what we are familiar with today.

How can huge continents move from one place to another?

The continents as well as the ocean floors rest on the asthenosphere beneath Earth's crust. Studies show that the asthenosphere is molten and moving, like a pot of thick, simmering soup. As the asthenosphere moves, it drags the continents and ocean floors with it.

Why are the moving sections called tectonic plates?

Continents move pretty slowly, usually only an inch or two (2 to 4 centimeters) a year.

The word *tectonic* comes from the Greek language and means "to put together or to take apart." The tectonic plates were responsible for the bringing together and breaking apart of Gondwanaland, Laurasia, and Pangaea. Tectonic plate movements, or shifts, cause the ocean floor to spread and the continents to travel. The six major **tectonic plates**, as the sections are called, are the African, American, Antarctic, Eurasian, Indian, and Pacific plates.

What makes the tectonic plates move?

Tectonic plates have several sources of energy. Early meteoric bombardment of Earth created heat, which was absorbed by Earth. Then, more heat has been, and is still, generated by radioactivity within Earth. And, we can't forget gravity and the pressure it puts on Earth's interior. These basic facts of heat and pressure cause the molten rock beneath Earth's crust to boil and flow. The crust on top of all this activity reacts with its own, more limited, movement.

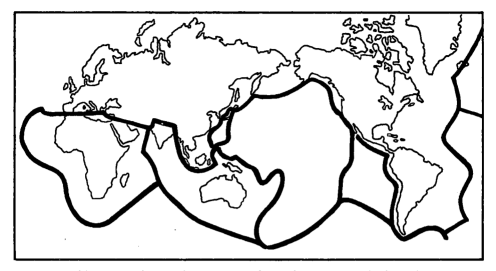

Earth's tectonic plates are huge sections of crust that move very slowly. As they move, they carry the continents with them. The edges of the plates are called plate margins. Most earthquakes and volcanoes occur at plate margins.

If the tectonic plates constantly move, why don't they bump into each other?

They do. When one plate collides with another, the point at which they meet is called the zone of contact. Plate collisions sometimes cause earthquakes or volcanic eruptions.

What happens when two tectonic plates meet?

Just like when two people meet or two football teams meet, almost anything can happen. Almost. There are a few typical occurrences depending on how the plates meet and what they are made of.

What happens when two continental plates collide?

When continental plates collide, the plate material gets folded and buckled up into mountain ranges. A good example of mountains formed this way are the Himalayas. These mountains have formed as the Indian-Australian plate crashes into the Eurasian plate. The continental plates share the same materials, just as two cars do. Imagine two cars colliding. What happens? The metal

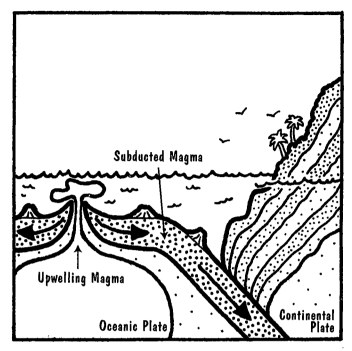

The material of Earth's crust is recycled over and over in a process that takes millions of years. At the midocean ridges, new crust is formed when magma wells up from beneath the ocean floor. Crust material gets drawn down into the mantle in ocean trenches, melts, and eventually comes to the surface again in volcanoes. Both ridges and trenches mark the edges of tectonic plates.

wrinkles and folds, forming mountains and valleys. Tectonic plates react the same way to impact, except that it is a very slow-motion collision, taking millions of years.

What happens when two oceanic plates collide?

In this case also the two plates consist of the same material. However, one oceanic plate is generally older and therefore heavier than the other plate. The older plate gets **subducted**, or pushed down, beneath the younger and more buoyant plate. The sinking plate gets heated up as it is subducted and remelts. With the increased pressure, the remelted material comes to the surface in volcanoes, forming island arcs. Japan is an example of land being formed when two oceanic plates collide.

What happens when an oceanic plate and a continental plate meet?

When an oceanic plate meets a continental plate, the oceanic plate gets subducted under the edge of the continental plate. This causes a huge trench to form at the boundary. The oceanic plate reheats and melts as it comes into contact with the molten mantle. The oceanic material comes back up because of pressure, forming volcanoes such as those along the west coast of South America.

Do tectonic plates always collide when they meet?

Sometimes, when two plates meet, they don't collide. If the plates are moving in the same direction, they will slide alongside each other.

Don't be fooled by the easy sound of the word *slide*, however. Whenever plates meet, there is great stress on the surface of Earth. When two plate edges meet and slide along each other, earthquakes occur. Rocks at the plate edges (called **faults**) may be pulverized into powder.

Such is the case along the San Andreas Fault in California, where some of the actual edges of the fault can be seen. Here, massive solid granite rocks are pressed together with the force of thousands of tons. Just about the only thing left after the plates meet is fine rock powder—and earthquakes.

Do we always feel the effects of tectonic plate collisions?

Not always. The shifting currents of molten rock in the mantle beneath them may make the plates press against each other or pull apart very, very slowly. Or the plates may move in the same direction along the same route, like two friends walking together.

Sooner or later, however, the continued pressure will force one of them to bend, dive, or rise. Even plates pressing against each other unnoticed will do so only until one finally breaks or snaps. Then, as untold tons of rock, soil, trees, buildings, roads, and all shift position— it's an earthquake.

What happens when plates pull apart?

When plates pull apart underwater, the hot magma instantly rises and spreads itself to form a new ocean floor. Under a continent, the crust splits open to allow magma out. The magma might make its way slowly to the surface, creating warm areas and hot springs or geysers as surface water meets it. Or the magma might explode, bringing into existence a new volcano where there was only cool earth before.

If the ocean floor spreads and opens, why doesn't water fall into the holes?

Water would, if it could. It can't however, because tremendous pressure forces molten rock from the mantle to erupt through the rifts and doesn't stop to allow in even a drip of water.

What are the chances of our continents splitting up further?

The chances are good, but most likely we won't be witnesses. These changes take hundreds, thousands, and millions of years.

Are mountains still growing?

For ages, people believed that Earth would always be the same. Now we realize that it is constantly changing.

The mighty Himalaya Mountains in South Asia, with their record-breaking heights, are still growing. The great Alps in Europe may grow taller still. On the other hand, the Rocky Mountains in the United States are continuing to wear away, just as the eastern Appalachians have diminished over time. These changes, however, generally take place at the rate of a pebble, a rock, or a boulder at a time.

What are glaciers?

Glaciers have created some of the most beautiful landscapes in the world.

When snow falls regularly in high mountains, it first runs into streams and rivers. But as the snow continues to fall, it cannot thaw fast enough and piles up. The pressure of the unmelted snow crushes the lower layers into ice, which then travels very slowly down the mountainside. This is a glacier.

What are fjords?

A dramatic feature of the Scandinavian, Scottish, and New Zealand landscapes, fjords are long, very steep valleys rising up from armlets of the sea. Glaciers created these deep, V-shaped gorges by cutting through the earth on their way to the sea. Fjords provide visual evidence of the incredible force of glaciers.

What are drumlins and eskers?

When glaciers melted after the Great Ice Age, they reshaped some parts of the landscape into mounds called drumlins. Drumlins can be several hundred yards (meters) long, and their length runs in the direction the ice was moving. A drumlin field may contain hundreds of these earthen mounds.

Similarly, eskers point in the direction the ice flowed, but they are longer and twist and turn like a raised earthen snake or stream. Tunnels of water carrying loads of sediment and debris formed under glaciers. When the glaciers melted, the rocks and silt were left as eskers, long winding streams of earth.

What are icebergs?

Icebergs are huge chunks of ice floating in the sea. These icebergs were pieces of glacier. Only the tip of an iceberg shows above water. Tons of glacial ice remain underwater, making icebergs particularly hazardous to ships.

Remember the Titanic! *On its first voyage, in 1912, the 46,000-ton (46,736-metric-ton) ocean liner— which was said to be unsinkable— hit an iceberg. It sank.*

How were glacial lakes formed?

The force and pressure of glaciers gouged out basins in the earth. At the time of melting, water collected in these interior depressions, forming wonderfully dramatic lakes. The melting of the glaciers also caused a great deal of flooding, which helped create glacial lakes.

What are moraines?

Glaciers of the Great Ice Age covered North America, Europe, and Asia. They gathered untold tons of earth along their paths. As they began to melt, they left behind rocks and sediment in huge mounds. Mounds left in front

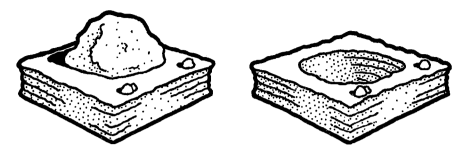

Glacial kettles form when a glacier leaves behind a block of ice and rock debris.
When the ice melts, a bowl-shaped depression is left in the ground.

of the glacier as it melted are called terminal moraines. Moraines left along the sides of a glacier as it melted are called lateral moraines. Kettle Moraine in Wisconsin is a glacial deposit in a depression left by a glacier.

What are glacial kettles?

Glacial kettles are the depressions the glaciers made when they left behind a block of ice surrounded by rock debris. The term designates a shape of the area.

Do glaciers still exist?

Yes. Glaciers can be found in mountain ranges such as the Alps in Europe and the Himalayas on the border of India and Tibet. Continental glaciers exist on Greenland and Antarctica. In fact, some scientists believe that this may not be the end of the Great Ice Age, but only a period of respite between ice ages. Ice may cover Earth again sometime in the future.

What are continental glaciers?

Glaciers form in places where the climate is cold enough for year-round snow. Instead of flowing down a mountainside, they creep over a great part of the land mass. Imagine being surrounded by ice and snow as far as you can see. That's probably what an ice age is like.

Greenland and Antarctica are the only two areas on Earth where continental glaciers remain. The glaciers are miles thick in the center and, under pressure, ooze over the landscape. The edges of the glacier are much thinner and sometimes extend into the ocean.

When did the Great Ice Age begin?

The last 3 million years have been filled with different ice ages and periods of warming. What we call the Great Ice Age began some 100,000 years ago and reached its peak about 18,000 years ago. During this time, great sheets of ice covered much of Earth's land. (This caused great migrations of living creatures as they moved ahead of the glaciers in search of warmer climates.)

How much land was ice-covered in the Great Ice Age?

Some 30 percent of the world's land was covered in ice, compared with 10 percent today. Ice covered a lot of the Northern Hemisphere, including Scandinavia, Great Britain, Northern Europe, and Russia. The Alpine glaciers covered much of France, Austria, southern Germany, and Italy. The Himalayan glaciers moved as far as Siberia. In the Southern Hemisphere, glaciers existed in the mountains of South America, Australia, and New Zealand. The Antarctic ice spread almost to the tip of South America.

When did the Great Ice Age end?

We may still be living in the end of it, or between ice ages. The glaciers and sheets of ice that covered many of the countries we know today, however, stopped their rampage about 12,000 years ago. A warmer climate prevailed, which melted the ice. The climate and extent of ice today stabilized—probably temporarily—about 6,000 years ago. That's not long ago, given the span of Earth's geological history: some 4 billion years.

How are caves formed?

Caves along seacoasts generally have been gouged out by water erosion. Most of these caves are made of limestone, a relatively soft rock. Waves crashing against rock face for hundreds, thousands, perhaps millions of years will wear away part of the rock. Depending on the force of the water, the composition of the rock, and the frequency of the waves, a cave may be created.

Inland caves are also formed by water erosion. Carbon dioxide, an element found in our atmosphere, mixes with rainwater to form a mild acid. The acidified rainwater makes its way through cracks in the limestone and, over time, carves caves from the rock.

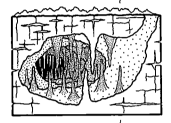

What are the long cone shapes in caves?

Three main rock forms are found in inland caves: columns, stalactites, and stalagmites. They are all created by the same process of erosion, only in reverse.

As the acidified rainwater cuts through the limestone, it retains limestone particles. When a drip from the ceiling of a cave falls constantly on the same spot, it leaves the limestone deposit behind. Over time this builds up into a cone shape, much like if you let sand run through your fist, it forms a cone. The deposits collect on both the ceiling and the floor of the cave where the drops continue to fall.

The cones hanging from the ceiling are called stalactites. The cones that seem to grow from the ground are stalagmites.

How are valleys created?

One way is by the force of glaciers bringing tons of ice and gouging out a valley between mountains. The current of rivers, created by snow and rain, will also cut a pathway through the earth. Over time—thousands and millions of years—the water will wear the earth down, making a valley.

How do islands come into being?

Islands are land masses completely surrounded by water. They range in size from a few feet of sand to a huge continent, such as Australia. Three basic activities will create an island. A piece of land may break off from a continental plate and float into the ocean or other body of water. (Australia, for example: Some 200 million years ago, when the supercontinent Pangaea split up, Australia gradually moved to its present position, as an island.) Or water may rise up and cut off a piece of land. (The Scilly Isles off the coast of England used to be attached to the mother country. As a result of flooding at the end of the last ice age, the sea level rose and cut off these granite islands.) Perhaps the most stupendous islands are those created by volcanic eruption. The molten layer of Earth, the mantle, pushes its way up through an oceanic plate. When it cools and solidifies, an island is left behind.

The Scillys (pronounced "sillies") were once a popular spot for pirates to hide out.

Are there some examples of volcanic islands?

One of the most romantic, and dangerous, examples is the chain of islands that form the state of Hawaii. These islands were created by volcanoes erupting from Earth's mantle. In fact, the smallest island is still growing as a result of molten rock continuing to spew up from beneath the ocean floor.

The Hawaiian Islands currently float over one of Earth's hotspots. The intense heat in that spot in the mantle results in volcanic activity, ultimately creating an island. A chain of islands is formed because the Pacific plate is slowly moving. As the plate shifts, the island on top is carried with it. Then, the new area over the **hotspot** will likely become home to another volcanic island.

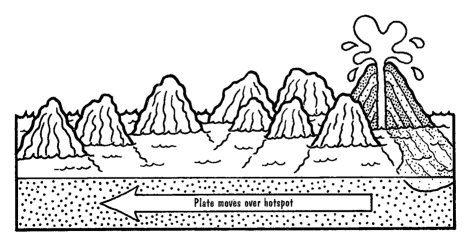

Plate moves over hotspot

The Hawaiian Islands formed over a hotspot, a place of high volcanic activity away from tectonic plate margins. Volcanoes over the hotspot gradually built up land masses that became islands. As the tectonic plate moves, it carries these islands away from the hotspot, and the volcanic activity on them decreases.

What is a hotspot?

Geologists have discovered 120 areas throughout the world with particularly intense activity in the molten layer of the mantle. Most of these hotspots are underwater, which makes sense since most of Earth is covered by water. Because the oceanic plates are constantly in motion, new islands may form when the old ones have moved on.

What are deserts?

We tend to think of deserts as hot stretches of sand as far as the eye can see. But, the term desert simply means a very dry climate, one that receives less than 10 inches (25 centimeters) of rain a year. Deserts can be made of rock, soil, stone, sand, or even ice. The Antarctic is considered a desert just as much as the Sahara.

What is sand?

Sand is a product of erosion. Rocks can be worn down by water or wind into the fine grains we call sand. Sandy deserts are filled with mountains of sand called dunes.

Earth's Ten Largest Deserts

Name	Location	Size (sq. miles)
Sahara	North Africa	3.5 million
Australian	Australia	1.3 million
Arabian	Arabian Peninsula	1 million
Turkmenistan	Central Asia	750,000
North America	Southwest U.S.	500,000
Patagonia	Argentina	260,000
Thar	India & Pakistan	230,000
Kalahari	Southwest Africa	220,000
Gobi	Mongolia & China	200,000
Takla Makan	China	200,000

How are sand dunes formed?

Wind keeps sand constantly on the move. When one grain is kicked up and falls back to the ground, its force knocks the next grain of sand into the air. Meanwhile the wind keeps blowing and more and more sand is launched.

Dunes tend to form around some barrier, such as a tree, boulder, or fence. When the wind pushes the sand against the obstruction, the grains fall and are blocked from further travel. More sand builds up until a mound, or dune, is created.

As the wind continues, sand is pushed up the face of the mound and just over the crest at the top. The dune then serves as a shelter from the wind, so piles of sand build up steeply on the windless, or leeward, side of the dune. These dunes can reach hundreds of feet (meters) high.

If the wind doesn't stop, the dune actually travels across the desert, or beach, as grains continually blow from one side, up over the crest, to the other. Dunes can travel more than 80 feet (24 meters) in a year in the desert.

What is desertification?

The process by which sand deserts invade other types of climates is called desertification. This is a serious problem for agricultural regions that border sand deserts. The sand is blown onto agricultural land, choking it until it can no longer produce vegetation.

hat is a volcano? ✦ What is magma? ✦ What is
lcano's physical structure? ✦ What is the stuf
at comes out of volcanoes? ✦ Are volcanic gase
ngerous? ✦ What do volcanic cinders and ash do
Wh__t __re pyroclastics? ✦ Besides spewin

VOLCANOES

lcani__ __at__, w__ __t __se_____ ____ ____g a
__ption__ ✦ W_____ ____ __ __ic bl__ck__? ✦ ____t is
lcanic bomb? ✦ Are there different kinds of lava
How hot is lava? ✦ How much lava comes out o
lcanoes? ✦ What are lava caves? ✦ What are lav
es? ✦ What is basalt? ✦ What is pumice?

What is a volcano?

A volcano is a gap in Earth's crust from which molten (melted) rock, ash, and steam flow—or burst, depending on the type of volcano and the pressure involved. **Volcanologists**—people who study volcanoes—have discovered several ways in which a volcano comes into existence. Some volcanoes occur at the edges of the huge tectonic plates that make up Earth's crust. When these plates collide, one gets pushed down underneath the other, or **subducted**. As the rocky material is subducted, it melts to form magma. This magma can burst up through the surface, creating a volcano. Other volcanoes form under the oceans, when magma gushes up from underneath the crust that makes up the ocean floor.

What is magma?

Magma is the term used for molten, or melted, rock. Magma wells up from the deep layer of Earth called the **mantle**. Rock in the mantle is partly melted because of the very high temperature at that depth. In some places, magma is closer to the surface of Earth than it is in other places. Because it is under great pressure, the magma oozes or gushes out of cracks in Earth's surface. To picture this, think of opening a can of soda that has been shaken. The magma is like the soda spraying out when you open the can. When magma comes to Earth's surface, it is called lava. The lava cools and solidifies—sometimes quickly, sometimes slowly—forming rocks.

What is a volcano's physical structure?

A volcano generally begins with a crack in Earth's crust. Deep below the surface, a magma chamber, a place where magma has collected, contains the molten rock before the volcano erupts. The magma comes to the surface through a vent, which is a long pipe or tunnel in the rock that acts as a chimney. In some volcanoes, the magma makes a depression, called a crater, when it reaches the surface. The crater fills with lava, which may harden in the crater or flow down the sides of the volcano. Over time, as a volcano explodes again and again, the falling lava and debris may build up to form a cone.

Different types of volcanoes have different shapes. Not all volcanoes explode, so not all have cones. Some have only slopes of hardened lava leading up to the crater's edge, because the lava flows out slowly.

What is the stuff that comes out of volcanoes?

In addition to lava, volcanoes produce gases, including steam, carbon and sulfur dioxides, carbon monoxide, and hydrogen chloride. Volcanoes also spew many different solids, such as cinders, ash, and pyroclastics, which are rocks that have been shattered by volcanic explosion. Bits of lava that have previously cooled also go flying.

Most solids result as the lava cools—in midair, in the ocean, or on land. Depending on the physical makeup of the lava and the environment surrounding the volcano, different solids are formed: basalt, pumice, obsidian, and various lava formations.

What do volcanic cinders and ash do?

In the great eruption of Mount Vesuvius on August 24, in the year A.D. 79, the people of Pompeii were killed—not by scalding lava, but by suffocating ash.

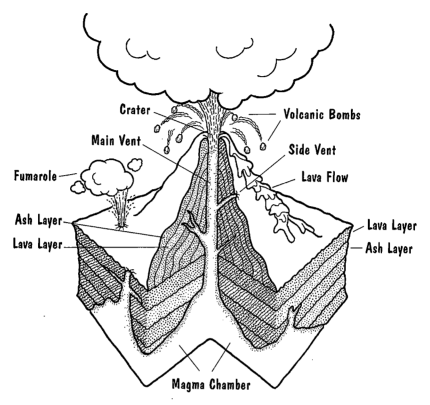

Crater

Main Vent

Volcanic Bombs

Side Vent

Fumarole

Lava Flow

Ash Layer

Lava Layer

Lava Layer

Ash Layer

Magma Chamber

This cross-section shows the different parts of a volcano. Not all volcanoes look like this—some are just cracks in the Earth's crust with magma rising up from underneath.

For 3 years, sunsets around the world were more highly colored as a result of all the ash Krakatoa threw into the atmosphere.

Cinders and ash are produced when bubbles of gas within the magma explode, causing the magma to fragment and shoot skyward. There the fragments cool into pellet formations. Clouds of ash and cinders can travel thousands of miles before falling to the ground. In August 1883, the midday eruption of Indonesia's Krakatoa—perhaps the most explosive in the last 10,000 years—produced so much ash that a thick layer coated an area of 300,000 square miles (800,000 square kilometers). The drifting clouds can also block out sunlight. The ash from Krakatoa darkened the sky in the region for two and a half days. Since sunlight produces so much of the world's energy, such experiences are not only frightening, but dangerous.

What are pyroclastics?

One of the first things an erupting volcano does is shoot a rain of shattered rock into the air. These fragments of rock are called pyroclastics, which means "shattered by fire." As they escape from underground, the gases combust when heated, exploding magma and any rock material into pyroclastics.

Besides volcanic material, what else does an eruption produce?

Flashes of lightning, flames, and the sound from the eruption can be detected from far away. The famous 1883 explosion of the island of Krakatoa in Indonesia was heard in Australia, about 2,400 miles (3,800 kilometers) away, 4 hours later!

The shape of land can change dramatically in a volcanic eruption. When Krakatoa exploded, an island disappeared. Before it exploded, the volcano's cone rose about 6,000 feet (1,800 meters) above sea level. Afterward, there was a basin in the ocean floor 4 miles (6 kilometers) across and two-thirds of a mile (one kilometer) deep. The volcano had caved in because the underlying material was gone, blown away as a huge volume of dust and ash. Eventually the erupting volcano built up a small island again, 2,667 feet (813 meters) high.

Tidal waves can result from volcanic eruption, destroying

Mount Vesuvius, Italy

Perhaps the most famous historical eruption took place in A.D. 79 in Italy. On the hot summer afternoon of August 24, the citizens living near the volcano went about their daily business. Vesuvius had been considered dormant or even extinct for generations. Suddenly one side of the volcano exploded. One observer, Pliny the Younger, described the ground shaking and tidal waves dashing the shores. A huge cloud of smoke hid the volcano's top. Pliny, who was about 18 miles (28 kilometers) away, could see flashes of lightning and flames. Explosion followed explosion. The inhabitants of the cities of Pompeii and Stabiae had no chance to escape as ash and steam rained down on them. Many were buried in midstride as they ran for protection, suffocated by the mounting debris. The city of Herculaneum was engulfed by waves of boiling mud. Lava, however, was strangely absent. The ruins of Pompeii were discovered by archaeologists in 1740, and artifacts from this once beautiful and prosperous city can be found in museums worldwide.

land and people. The 120-foot (36-meter) wave produced by Krakatoa's explosion hit the islands of Sumatra and Java, killing some 36,000 people.

Volcanic activity can also create earthquakes, avalanches, landslides, and mudslides.

What are volcanic blocks?

These are large chunks of material catapulted from volcanoes. The volcano known as Stromboli, in the Mediterranean Sea near Sicily, Italy, has thrown blocks weighing 2 tons (1.8 metric tons) a distance of 2 miles (3.2 kilometers). Volcanoes have been known to throw blocks as high as 50 miles (80 kilometers) in the air—about 10 times higher than a passenger jet flies.

What is a volcanic bomb?

A mass of lava thrown into the air may become rounded or tear-shaped as it falls to the ground. It cools as it falls, but may not completely harden. Volcanic bombs do not really explode when they hit, but the still-molten interior splatters on the ground.

Are there different kinds of lava?

The two most prevalent types of lava worldwide, pahoehoe (pronounced pa-*hoy*-hoy) and aa (pronounced *ah*-ah), take their names from the native Hawaiian language. The state of Hawaii is actually a chain of volcanic islands, where pahoehoe and aa are both found in abundance.

Mount Tambora, Indonesia

Tambora's eruption began on April 5, 1815, and did not stop until July. Troops who were sent to investigate the early rumblings believed the sounds came from pirates attacking military bases. The worst came on April 11 and 12, and the volcano's explosions could be heard 1,000 miles (1,600 kilometers) away. Darkness fell at noon up to 300 miles (480 kilometers) away, a result of airborne volcanic ash and debris. The following year, known as "the year without summer," the effects of Tambora reached the northeastern United States and Western Europe. Crops failed and livestock died due to the intense cold. In the northeastern United States, snow fell all summer. Famine threatened the Northern Hemisphere—all because of a volcanic eruption in Indonesia. Volcanologists believe that Tambora's eruption could easily have been the worst in 10,000 years.

Pahoehoe has the shape of thick cords of rope or puffy billows. It can look something like black whipped cream. When highly fluid lava flows, the outer surface area congeals to form a thin, flexible exterior. The lava inside continues to run, molding the outside layer into ropelike forms. These shapes remain when the entire mass solidifies.

Aa results from oozing semisolid lava. As aa flows, it carries rough, jagged shards of rock along its path. Aa hardens into sharp, splintery, knifelike edges. You can walk comfortably on cold pahoehoe barefoot, but aa will slice the soles of your shoes.

How hot is lava?

Exit temperatures—the temperature of lava as it comes from the mouth, or crater, of volcanoes—indicate that lava's heat varies. The temperature ranges from 700 to 1,200° Celsius (1,300 to 2,200° Fahrenheit). At its hottest, lava is about 10 times the temperature of boiling water. It also ranges in viscosity, or how thick or runny it is. Lava can be very thin and fluid, or it can be so thick that it almost doesn't flow.

What are lava caves?

After the surface of flowing lava has hardened, it sometimes forms a tunnel through which liquid lava streams. When the inner river of lava flows away, the tunnel remains hollow, like a cavern or cave. Lava caves can even have stalactites (cone shapes hanging

Pele, Hawaiian Goddess of Volcanoes

According to Hawaiian folklore, the powerful goddess Pele lives inside the islands' volcanoes. When angered, Pele sends streams of molten lava down a volcano's slopes, burning everything: houses, trees, and people.

Pele's sister, Namaka the ocean goddess, meets Pele along the shoreline. Sometimes their meeting is quiet, as lava gently flows into the water. But sometimes their encounter causes the ocean waters to boil, sending up huge clouds of steam and smoke.

Human sacrifice was believed to quiet Pele's anger, and islanders threw their neighbors into the mouths of volcanic craters to calm her down. Nowadays, however, those wishing to appease the volcano goddess throw *oleho* berries into the craters' bubbling lava instead. The last human being was sacrificed to Pele in 1819.

The estimated daily lava production of Mauna Loa plus Kiluaea, 2 large volcanoes in Hawaii, would fill 65,000 cement trucks.

from the ceiling) and stalagmites (cone shapes rising from the floor) just like limestone caves.

What are lava lakes?

Trapped by the terrain into depressions or pools, lava may remain fluid rather than solidifying. These lava lakes may be fed with new hot lava pouring up from below Earth's surface. Sooner or later, the lava's channel collapses, stopping the flow of more lava. Shallow lava lakes may harden after a year, but the deepest ones—up to 400 feet deep (about 120 meters)—can take a quarter of a century to cool and harden completely. Some, however, disappear, sucked back down into their craters like water down a drain.

What is pumice?

Pumice, called the "featherweight of rocks," is another form of solid lava. It looks like brown-gray bits of soapsuds frozen together. Pumice is light enough to float on water because it is chock full of holes, evidence of gas bubbles.

What is obsidian?

Also called volcanic glass, obsidian is black, sharp-edged shards of hardened lava. Early *homo sapiens* used obsidian for tools.

How do volcanoes create black sand?

The famous black sand beaches of Hawaii result when the fiery, black basaltic lava of Mauna Kea shatters upon contact with the ocean. Water erosion from the ocean's waves helps to grind these basaltic fragments into fine sand.

Are there different kinds of volcanoes?

Although each volcano is unique, there are four main types of volcanoes, based on shape: shield, cinder cone, composite, and lava cone. Hawaii's Mauna Loa is a typical shield volcano. Paricutín, in Mexico, exemplifies a cinder cone volcano. The image of a volcano most of us carry around in our minds is a composite type, such as Mount Fuji in Japan. And California's Lassen Peak typifies the gentler lava cone volcano.

What causes the different shapes of volcanoes?

A volcano's shape is determined by the type of eruption, the environment (other rock formations in the area and their chemical makeup), and the makeup of the volcanic materials. Explosive eruptions may blow off the tops of volcanoes in a flash, while gentle flows of lava build sloping cones over long periods of time.

How is a shield volcano created?

A steady flow of thin, basaltic lava from a number of relatively small vents creates a shield volcano. The magma may appear in fiery fountains, filling the volcano's crater and overflowing. Shield volcanoes do not make mountains or cones. They rise gently over the vent and spread out widely, resembling an upside-down plate.

How is a cinder cone volcano formed?

Cinder cone volcanoes explode abruptly, building very steep, but not very tall, slopes. Far underground, the magma combines with water and gases to form a bubbly mixture. As it approaches the surface, the reduced pressure causes the gas bubbles to explode, throwing debris high into the air. The larger fragments tend to fall on the slopes, building them up further. The smaller pieces are carried on the winds. Additional lava may make its way out near the base of the cone after the initial explosion.

What is a composite volcano?

Composite volcanoes are made of a variety of materials. A hardened piece of magma may plug up the vent and be blown out by the built-up gases below. Fragments of ash and cinder shoot into the air accompanied by lava that flows down the slopes. The cone, therefore, will have

Pumice

You probably experience the benefit of volcanoes every day without even knowing it. Every time you brush your teeth, you may be putting volcanic rock in your mouth. Pumice—the highly porous, feather-light volcanic rock—is also a mild abrasive often used in toothpaste and scouring powders. You can find pieces of pumice for sale in most health and beauty stores as it is helpful in scrubbing away calluses.

Ten Most Recent Major Eruptions

Volcano	Place	Year
Augustine	Alaska, U.S.	1986
Ruiz	Colombia	1985
El Chichón	Mexico	1983
St. Helens	Washington, U.S.	1980
Nyirangongo	Zaire	1977
Helgafell	Iceland	1973
Kilauea	Hawaii, U.S.	1969
Agung	Indonesia	1963
Surtsey	Iceland	1963
Capelinhos	Azores	1957

alternating layers of ash, cinder, and lava, as each falls and hardens on top of the other. Composite volcanoes tend to have dramatic, steep summits sloping down to wide, softer-looking bases of hardened lava.

How is a lava cone volcano produced?

A lava cone is, perhaps, the simplest type of volcano: Lava pours from one vent and quickly hardens.

Are there different kinds of volcanic eruptions?

Volcano eruptions are classified by volcanologists in one of five ways, from most to least violent: Pelean, Vulcanian, Strombolian, Hawaiian, or Icelandic. The names of the classifications come from specific volcanoes or places where volcanoes have erupted.

What is a Pelean eruption like?

Gases, steam, pumice, and ash are the major players in Pelean eruptions. The great strength of the explosion is a result of hardened magma stopping up the crater. Underneath, heat and pressure grow until the magma plug blows. Then gases, steam, frothy pumice, and ash rocket skyward. Lava appears only after the build-up of other materials has been released. Pelean eruptions are named after Mount Pelée on the island of Martinique, in the Caribbean Sea.

What is a Vulcanian eruption?

A Vulcanian eruption may spew gases, pumice, and ash, like a Pelean eruption. In this case, however, magma in the volcano's crater has only partially hardened to a thick, hot glop that inhibits the release of interior gases. When sufficient heat and pressure have built up, the

Pelean

Hawaiian

Vulcanian

Strombolian

Volcanoes vary in shape and in how they erupt. Eruptions can be slow, as in volcanoes in Hawaii, or they can happen very suddenly, like a Pelean eruption.

magma, gases, ash, and pumice shoot into the sky, falling back down like hot rain. This kind of eruption was named for the volcano Vulcan, near Sicily, Italy.

What happens in a Strombolian eruption?

Named after the Italian volcano Stromboli—also known as the Lighthouse of the Mediterranean—these eruptions are identified by large flying globs of lava inter-mittently shooting from the volcano's crater. Encrusted magma thinly blocks the crater's mouth, allowing pressure within to escape at regular intervals, lobbing lava into the air. Most of the lava and other debris falls back down into the crater. Because they can be seen for miles, these flash-

Hawaiian Islands, United States

The Hawaiian volcanoes could be said to be more creative than destructive. Volcanic activity built this chain of islands, and the only known deadly eruptions killed a division of the Hawaiian army—in 1790—and one other person—in 1924. The 1969 eruption took no lives. Four shield volcanoes make up the island of Hawaii. Mauna Kea first grew to 13,825 feet (4,200 meters) above water. The smaller volcanoes, Kilauea and Haulalai, then sprouted from its sides. Further internal volcanic activity then created Mauna Loa, 13,678 feet (4,169 meters) in the air. The mild nature of these volcanoes allowed the United States to open them, and Haleakala on nearby Maui, as the Hawaii Volcanoes National Park. Since 1911, the Hawaiian Volcano Observatory on Hawaii has gathered an immense amount of data and information on volcanology, the study of volcanoes.

es of lava from Stromboli have guided sailors through the Mediterranean Sea for centuries.

How can a Hawaiian eruption be described?

A Hawaiian eruption may begin with lava spewing up from a fissure (a long crack) in Earth's surface. This fissure will seal up, leaving only the few vents typical of a shield volcano. The gas content of the magma is relatively low, which makes the lava less explosive. Generally, the lava flows rapidly over the volcano's slopes. Hawaiian eruptions were named for the immense shield volcanoes of Hawaii.

What is an Icelandic eruption?

In these mildest of eruptions, lava flows from fissures in Earth's crust many miles long. The flooding basaltic lava spreads out in sheets to form amazing plateaus. Iceland is the only place where these eruptions have occurred in recorded history.

What is the difference between a crater and a caldera?

The opening in the top of a volcano for the passage of lava, ash, and cinders is known as the crater. This crater may fall in on itself as the lava weakens it. Or, an explosive eruption may take off the top of the crater. In either case, a much larger depression is created at the top of the volcano, and this is called a caldera. Calderas may be thousands of feet wide and hundreds of feet deep.

What is a fumarole?

A crack may appear on a volcano's cone or slope above a stream of lava that is contained within the volcano. Steam and hot gases—often noxious, or poisonous—shoot out of the opening, forming a jet stream of vapor called a fumarole.

How do volcanoes create hot springs?

Streams of magma heat groundwater until it boils up to the surface in hot springs. The heat can also be generated from cooling volcanic material or the friction of tectonic plates moving against each other.

Steam Heat

In Iceland, just south of the Arctic Circle, underground pipes channel volcanic steam to homes and other buildings for warmth. On a grander scale, geothermal power (literally "earth-warmth") is harnessed by tapping underground areas of highly pressurized steam and funneling it into great turbines that produce electricity.

What causes a geyser?

When an underground hot spring forms a long tunnel up to the surface, pressure prevents the water from boiling. Instead, the water becomes superheated—hotter than boiling but without the formation of bubbles—until it flashes instantly into steam. At that point, it shoots up through the tunnel, creating a tall fountain of steam and hot water on Earth's surface—a geyser.

What is the largest active volcano in the world?

Mauna Loa, part of the Hawaiian Islands, rises some 33,000 feet (10,000 meters) from the ocean floor to claim the title of largest active volcano. Mauna Loa is actually one of four connected shield volcanoes that make up the island of Hawaii. Mauna Loa's neighbor, Mauna Kea, is the largest inactive volcano worldwide, rising some 32,000 feet (9,700 meters) from the ocean floor. Its peak is usually snowcapped.

How can lakes of water form in volcanic craters?

Volcanoes go through periods of activity. They may not be active for thousands, even millions, of years. In time, rainwater and melted snow can accumulate inside the crater, making a clear, beautiful lake. Crater Lake in Oregon came into existence after the top of Mount Mazama collapsed and formed a huge caldera. The caldera filled with water, creating an impressive lake at the top of the volcano's steeply sloping sides.

Do volcanoes appear where none existed before?

Yes. For instance, on February 20, 1943, a few wisps of smoke appeared in a cornfield in the Mexican state of Michoacán. Soon, lava and ash were spouting from an expanding vent that simply opened up in the ground. By the next day the cone was already 160 feet (50 meters) high. In just one year, the cone of a new volcano—Paricutín—stood 1,475 feet (450 meters) from its base.

The Island of Surtsey, off the coast of Iceland, was created by a volcano that began erupting in November 1963. Surtsey began its life as a towering plume of smoke and water that boiled up from the depths of the ocean. Day after day, smoke, flame, and ash shot out of the water until—within 3½ years—a cone of cinders and ash had built up an island 1 square mile (2.5 square kilometers) in area and 560 feet (171 meters) above sea level. After that, the main volcanic activity quieted down. The island is now inhabited by plants and animals, and Icelandic and U.S. scientists have jointly established a biological research program there.

When is a volcano considered active?

An active volcano shows signs of stirring. This may come in the form of tremors, escaping clouds of smoke or gases, minor eruptions, or any activity within the past century. Of course, an erupting volcano is very active.

What is a dormant volcano?

A dormant, or sleeping, volcano is one that has not erupted or shown signs of activity for centuries. Consider, however, that when Mount Vesuvius buried 16,000 people in A.D. 79, it would have been considered dormant. Even if a volcano is dormant for a long time, that doesn't mean it's gone for good.

When is a volcano considered extinct?

An extinct volcano, if such a thing exists—and only time will tell—is a truly dead volcano. There are no signs of activity; the volcano isn't located in an area of likely activity; and there is no historic record of activity in ages. Scientists know, however, that given the constant movement of Earth's plates and the magma below them, an extinct volcano might always roar back into life.

Can volcanic eruptions be predicted?

Volcanoes are mostly unpredictable. There are, however, some means of detection and prediction, both natural and scientific.

Close observance of the area around a volcano can provide important signals. Clouds of steam or smoke may arise from the volcano's crater. The ground may rumble. There may be minor shudders or earthquakes. The increased temperature of nearby streams, springs, and even surface rocks may give a clue. Rock slides or avalanches from the volcano's cone or slopes provide evidence of possible eruption. However, all these things may happen without further volcanic activity.

Scientists have developed various instruments to measure predictors of volcanic eruption. The ground may tilt slightly before an eruption; a tiltmeter measures this activity. Seismographs, commonly used in recording earthquakes, can also be used to gauge the rumblings that sometimes come before an eruption. Rising magma distorts Earth's natural electric currents and

Volcano Protection Plans

The best protection against volcanic destruction is to stay far away. That may be impossible, since volcanoes can appear almost anywhere, but it isn't likely one will pop up in your backyard as one did in Paricutín, Mexico. There are, however, some ways to try and reduce the inevitable damage from volcanic eruptions. Channels can be built to direct the flow of lava away from populated areas. Levees, dams, and dikes can be erected to contain the flow of lava and mud. Artificial earthworks, such as mounds, can provide high ground for refugees. Water is sometimes poured extensively over lava flows to encourage solidification. The U.S. Air Force has bombed lava flows in Hawaii with some success in preventing rampant destruction.

magnetic field. A restivity meter and a magnetometer note these changes. Thermometers register changing temperatures in the surrounding environment, which may precede volcanic eruptions.

Despite all of these ways to monitor volcanoes, eruptions and explosions are difficult to predict. For example, in 1980, scientists thought that Mount Saint Helens—a dormant volcano in Washington State—was preparing for a *mild* eruption. They were taken by surprise. On the morning of May 18, the volcano blew its top, spewing clouds, lava, ash, and rocks; causing avalanches, mudslides, and floods; and registering moderate earthquakes between 3 and 5 on the Richter scale. (The Richter scale measures the magnitude of earthquakes on a scale of 0 to 9.0.) More than 60 people died and about 200 were left homeless. The damage and destruction covered more than 200 square miles (518 square kilometers).

Where are volcanoes located?

Some places on Earth are especially likely to have volcanic activity. Most of these sites mirror where Earth's tectonic plates come together and move apart.

The Pacific region hosts the largest concentration of volcanoes, called the "ring of fire." There are also volcanoes in the Mediterranean Sea, Africa, and the Atlantic Ocean.

Throughout the world there are places called hotspots. Scientists have determined that these areas, while not necessarily residing over the edges of tectonic plates, show accelerated magma movement and heat. They are also likely places for volcanoes to erupt.

What is the ring of fire?

This region of great volcanic activity rings the Pacific Ocean. The Pacific tectonic plate, which lies under most of the ocean, meets several other plates at its edges. These tectonic plates are moving very, very slowly. Where the plates meet, they collide or slide past each other. The result is earthquakes and volcanoes.

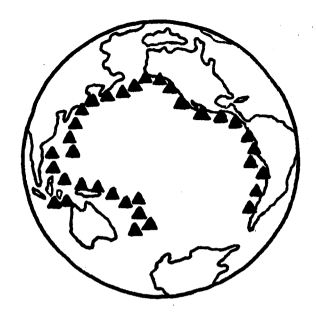

Most volcanoes and earthquakes occur in an area
that rings the Pacific Ocean. Volcanoes and earthquakes happen in other places, too, but they are
most common in this area, called the ring of fire.

The ring of fire lines the coastal lands and waters of
New Zealand, Papua New Guinea, Indonesia, the Philip-
pines, Japan, the Kamchatka Peninsula of Russia, the
Aleutian Islands, and western North and South America.

How many active volcanoes exist in the world?

Given that some underwater volcanoes may erupt
without detection and that dormant or even extinct volcanoes may come back to life, we cannot count the exact
number of active volcanoes worldwide. That does not
stop scientists from estimating, however. We know of
some 350 volcanoes along the Pacific Ocean's tectonic
plate and up to an additional 600 elsewhere, for a total of
approximately 950 volcanoes around the world. The most
conservative estimate reports 600 volcanoes.

Top Ten Deadly Eruptions

Volcano	Place	Fatalities	Year
Tuxtla	Mexico	50,000	1793
Krakatoa	Indonesia	36,000	1883
Pelée	Martinique	26,000	1902
Ruiz	Colombia	22,000	1985
Etna	Italy	20,000	1669
Vesuvius	Italy	16,000	79
Etna	Italy	15,000	1169
La Soufrière	Martinique	15,000	1902
Tambora	Indonesia	14,000	1815
Santa Maria	Guatemala	6,000	1902

Are there any benefits from volcanic eruptions?

As with most of the phenomena we call natural disasters, we benefit as well as suffer from volcanoes. One major positive result of a volcanic eruption is soil enrichment. When lava decays and crumbles, nutrients—such as phosphate, calcium, and potash—leach, or seep, into the ground. The porous nature of volcanic debris provides good drainage. Years after an eruption, lush forests, crops, and gardens can grow on the previously barren land.

Volcanoes are important valves through which Earth's interior pressure escapes. Without this release, pressure might build up to an unbearable limit, which could result in a far more destructive explosion.

Volcanic heat and activity underground have a part in the formation of precious gems and metals. The shifts in Earth's surface that accompany volcanoes help to bring these riches to the surface.

Scientifically, volcanoes teach us a great deal about Earth: its temperature, pressure, and substance. We have also gained a greater understanding of tectonic plate movement by watching volcanic activity. Since volcanoes played an important role in the formation of our ocean and atmosphere—two critical factors for life's creation and survival—they may hold answers to how life began.

w does an earthquake happen? ❖ How long doe
earthquake last? ❖ What are aftershocks?
hat are faults? ❖ Are there different kinds o
ults? ❖ What do faults look like? ❖ Where is th
n Andreas Fault? ❖ In what parts of the worl

EARTHQUAKES

n earthquakes be measured? ❖ How does
ismograph work? ❖ What is the Richter scale?
hat is the modified Mercalli scale? ❖ How man
rthquakes occur annually? ❖ Where do mos

How does an earthquake happen?

The ground we walk on is actually the surface of a number of separate thick plates of solid rock which rest on Earth's mantle of melted rock. We know that our present continents were created by the movements of these plates, coming together and splitting apart. (The plates are called tectonic plates; *tectonic* means "coming together and breaking apart.") The plates continue to move and, consequently, they sometimes run into each other, slide against each other, and slip one on top of the other. This underground movement is sometimes reflected on the surface of Earth by earthquakes.

While tectonic plates are constantly moving, they usually move very slowly. The crust of Earth does not reflect every movement, but stores up the energy from the movement inside its rocks until they can no longer bear the strain. At that point, the energy is released through the weakest points in Earth's crust, causing the ground to suddenly move: earthquakes.

How long does an earthquake last?

If you count tremors prior to the quake and aftershocks, earthquakes can last for months. But the central event lasts only seconds or minutes.

As a result of the Missouri quake in 1811 (the strongest earthquake ever to hit the continental United States) the Mississippi River changed its course.

The great San Francisco earthquake of 1906 began when the ground shuddered for about a minute at 5:11 A.M., April 18. Ten seconds of quiet followed. At 5:12 A.M., the major quake—7.9 on the Richter scale—began. Three minutes later, it was over, leaving thousands of buildings in pieces, broken gas mains, buckled streets, and raging fires. Ultimately, 75 percent of the city was destroyed.

The disastrous earthquake in Mexico City on the morning of September 19, 1985, also lasted 3 minutes. In that time, 250 buildings were leveled. The next day another quake destroyed another 150 buildings and put a stop to the first earthquake's relief work.

The Ten Most Deadly Earthquakes

Place	Date	Fatalities	Richter
Shenshu, China	1556	830,000	
Tangshan, China	1976	650,000	7.6
Calcutta, India	1737	300,000	
Tokyo, Japan	1803	200,000	
China	1927	200,000	
Kansu, China	1920	180,000	8.6
Tokyo and Yokohama, Japan	1857	107,000	8.3
Messina, Italy	1908	73,000	7.5
China	1932	70,000	

What are aftershocks?

Just as earthquakes are often preceded by quieter tremors, they are commonly followed by aftershocks. These relatively minor quakes occur as the crust's rock readjusts after releasing its pent-up energy. Aftershocks can be as devastating as the main quake, or even more so. They frequently finish off the destruction of areas weakened in the initial shock.

What are faults?

Scientists call the places where earth movement has left cracks in the surface rock faults. Since earthquakes happen at places where two tectonic plates touch, or converge, quakes will recur in the same area time and again.

For instance, the San Andreas Fault in the United States is a 650-mile (1,040-kilometer) long, 20-mile (32-kilometer) deep fracture in Earth's crust running from the Mexican border northward into California. It is the area where the North American tectonic plate and the Pacific Ocean plate collide.

Are there different kinds of faults?

Faults are classified three different ways: normal, reverse, and strike-slip. **Normal faults** are no more normal than the others, though they were once thought to be. They occur when the end of one plate slides vertically down the end of another. A **reverse fault** describes the

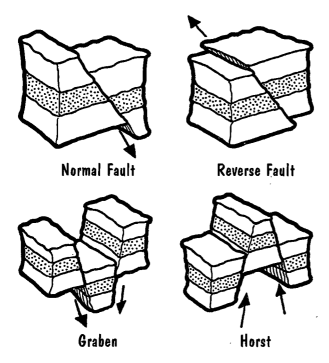

Normal Fault   Reverse Fault

Graben   Horst

Different earthquake faults cause distinctive land formations. Normal and reverse faults result in ridges. Sections of land between two faults are called horsts when land is thrust upwards and grabens when it drops down.

opposite motion: when one plate end moves vertically up the end of another plate. A **strike-slip fault** appears when two plate ends slide past each other horizontally. Plate movements can be both vertical and horizontal at the same time, producing what is known as an **oblique fault**.

What do faults look like?

Normal and reverse faults, one plate end sliding vertically down or up another, create long ridges. A **graben**, or long trench, is produced by two reverse faults running side by side. A **horst**, a long ridge or plateau, is formed by two normal faults parallel to each other. Strike-slip faults shift the earth horizontally, moving one side of the fault along the other side. If two stop signs face each other across a strike-slip fault, after an earthquake, one of the signs may have moved many feet to the right or left of the other.

Where is the San Andreas Fault?

Complex movements of Earth's tectonic plates created the San Andreas Fault inland from the coast of California. It extends north and south through much of the state and is intersected by other faults, such as the Hayward Fault near San Francisco and the Garlock Fault near Los Angeles.

The San Andreas Fault is a result of the North Pacific plate and the North American plate slipping past each other. Some 30 million years ago, the land we call California was just west of the western Mexican coast. Some 30 million years in the future, it may be off the west coast of Canada. If the two plates were slipping past each other smoothly, earthquakes would not be so common. The edges of the two plates, however, make contact. Where they meet, the solid rock of Earth's crust must adjust to the pressure and friction. When the solid rock can no longer bear the stress, rock breaks, and an earthquake begins.

Ten Most Recent Major Earthquakes			
Place	Date	Fatalities	Richter
Sea of Japan	1993	97	7.8
Erzincan, Turkey	1992	4,000	6.2
Iran	1990	60,000	7.7
San Francisco, California	1989		7.1
Mexico City, Mexico	1985	10,000	7.8
Morgan, California	1984		6.1
Coalinga, California	1983		6.5
Iran	1981	8,000	
Italy	1980	4,800	
Iran	1978	25,000	

In what parts of the world do earthquakes happen?

There are parts of the world considered geographically stable zones and parts of the world prone to earthquakes. If you've read about volcanoes, it won't surprise you that one of the major earthquake areas is along the rim of the Pacific Ocean, the same locale as the volcanic ring of fire. An earthquake belt also extends from the mountains around the Mediterranean Sea east through Iran and the Himalaya Mountains into China. East Africa has one of the longest inland earthquake zones, extending 3,600 miles (5,760 kilometers), called the East African Rift. Northern Afghanistan and Tadzhikistan suffer numerous intermediate quakes. Another area of earthquakes sweeps from the Mideast through the Caucasus Mountains into northern Turkey.

Why does the Pacific Rim have so many earthquakes and volcanoes?

Earthquakes and volcanoes both signal Earth's tectonic plate movements, or land shifts. The internal movements of these plates show up mostly in areas around the edges of the plates.

The large Pacific plate, under the Pacific Ocean, seems to be very active—it may even be rotating. The stress created where the oceanic plate meets the various continental plates around the Pacific Rim is commonly released in earthquakes and volcanoes.

Up to one million earthquakes are recorded every year. Although every single quake alters Earth's crust, most of them are noticed only by seismographs.

Can earthquakes be measured?

Earthquakes themselves can be measured in terms of strength, duration, and location. Various scientific instruments and comparative scales have been developed for these purposes. The seismograph measures all three. The Richter scale describes an earthquake's strength, or intensity.

Of course, the destruction caused by earthquakes can be measured in many other ways: injuries, fatalities, homelessness; cost of damage, cost of reconstruction, time it takes to reconstruct; consequent fires and power outages; costs to businesses and the government; cost of earthquake insurance; days out of school; and much more.

How does a seismograph work?

Seismographs depend on one of the laws of motion developed by Isaac Newton, who lived from 1642 to 1727. The law basically states that any object at rest tends to stay at rest until it is moved.

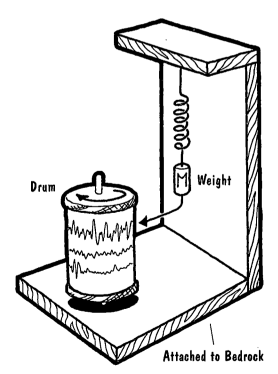

Drum   Weight

Attached to Bedrock

Seismographs are the instruments scientists most often use to measure and study earthquakes.

A simple seismograph consists of a heavy weight that hangs free and a revolving drum covered in paper on which Earth's movements are recorded. The drum is solidly fastened to bedrock. When an earth tremor occurs, the drum moves. The weight, however, remains steady, and a marker attached to it draws on the paper (already marked in segments of time), as the drum jiggles. When the drum moves, because the bedrock is moving, the marker draws wavelike lines. The more the drum moves, the larger the wavy marks grow.

The most modern seismographs respond to Earth's natural electrical currents, which are disturbed by tremors, to move the drum. The electrical signals can be amplified to record even the slightest movements. Lasers and light-sensitive paper replace the markers and regular paper, thereby cutting down on distortion caused by the friction of a marker actually touching the paper's surface.

The Modified Mercalli Scale

The modified Mercalli scale is an early system used to designate the intensity of earthquakes. Invented in 1902 by the Italian seismologist Giuseppe Mercalli, the scale was later modified by American scientists Harry O. Wood and Frank Neumann. The Mercalli scale is based primarily on people's experiences of earthquakes. The scale goes from I to XII (the Roman numerals for 1 and 12), with I described as "not felt except by a few people" and XII, "damage total." Level III reads "felt quite noticeably indoors, especially on upper floors of buildings," and VII says "everyone runs outdoors."

What is the Richter scale?

The Richter scale was developed in the 1940s by American scientists Beno Gutenberg and Charles Richter in order to gauge scientifically the intensity of individual earthquakes. The idea behind the Richter scale is that the energy released by an earthquake should be measured, not its effect on Earth's surface. The Richter scale provides an accepted standard of measurement, based on seismographic recordings.

The Richter scale ranges from 0 to 9.0. Earthquakes of 2 or lower are imperceptible. The 9.0 ceiling is simply a reflection of how intense earthquakes have been in the

Earthquakes greater than 8.9 release energy millions of times greater than the first atomic bomb.

Earthquake Myths

Earthquakes appear in the mythology of many cultures. This makes sense since most of the populated areas of the world have experienced earthquakes. Often, Earth is said to be carried on the back of an animal, such as a tortoise, dragon, fish, or frog. Earthquakes resulted from the animal's movement.

Ancient Greek philosophers had various earthquake theories, which depended on what they thought Earth was made of. One said that Earth's interior was caving in; the inside of Earth must be empty. Still another maintained that fire inside Earth caused the tremors. Another said tremors were felt when the winds inside Earth rushed about.

The Roman poet Ovid claimed that earthquakes occurred when Earth got too close to the Sun and trembled from the star's great heat and radiance.

Earthquakes have often been blamed on people. People's sinfulness would anger the gods so much that an earthquake would be sent as punishment.

Even in more scientific times, people blamed others for earthquakes. In Boston, Benjamin Franklin was accused of tempting quakes by putting up his new invention: lightning rods.

Perhaps most surprising is that some of these theories cite factors—such as fire, water, and electricity—that arise in the scientific study of earthquakes.

past. If there were to be an earthquake stronger than any before, the scale would reach higher to encompass it.

One important element of this scale is that the levels increase exponentially. Each notch up the scale represents 10 times the motion and 30 times the energy of the previous level. For example, an earthquake registering 7.5 has 10 times the ground motion and 30 times the released energy of a 6.5 earthquake. An 8.5 earthquake has 100 times the ground motion and 900 times the released energy of a 6.5 quake.

Where do most earthquakes register on the Richter scale?

Seismologists, people who study earthquakes, estimate that more than 600,000 tremors occur annually without anyone knowing (less than 2.0 on the Richter scale). Another 300,000 register on seismographs (2.0–2.9), but still no one feels them. Some 49,000 quakes are noticed only by people living near their epicenters, where the quakes reach the surface (3.0–3.9). Slight, localized damage occurs in about 6,000 minor shocks every year (4.0–4.9). Moderate quakes happen an average of 1,000 times a year (5.0–5.9). About 120 large shocks, destructive only in populated areas, take place annually (6.0–6.9). Major earthquakes, causing serious damage and recorded worldwide, happen at a rate of only 14 a year (7.0–7.9), while great earthquakes that cause complete destruction near their epicenters occur once every 5 to 10 years (8.0–8.9). The largest earthquakes, such as the 1964 Good Friday quake in Alaska, will take place once or twice within a century (9.0 and up).

What is the epicenter of an earthquake?

Earthquakes begin inside Earth and the energy ripples outward in all directions: toward the surface, toward Earth's core, and all around. If the earthquake's energy reaches the surface, that point of surfacing is called the epicenter.

Where is an earthquake's focus?

Scientists call an earthquake's point of origin—inside Earth—the focus. It represents a sudden snap or readjustment of materials either deep within the Earth or just below its surface.

How deep within Earth can a quake begin?

Earthquakes have been found to occur at almost any level within Earth. Shallow disturbances take place just below the surface, while intermediate quakes begin several miles within Earth's crust. The focuses of deep earthquakes have been registered as deep as 400 miles (640 kilometers) underground.

What happens in an earthquake between the focus and the epicenter?

Two tectonic plates shift within Earth at the focus of the earthquake. The energy released by their movement

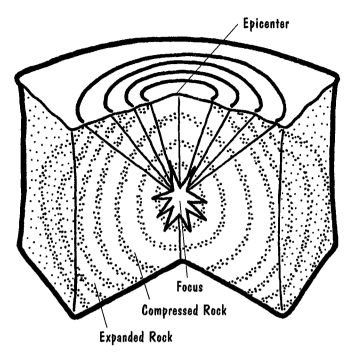

An earthquake's focus marks where underground rock can no longer bear the stress of Earth's internal shifts. Shock waves travel out from the focus, causing adjacent rock to expand and compress as the earthquake's energy passes through. The epicenter of the quake is where the shock waves break through Earth's surface.

ripples outward to the surrounding rock in waves, called earthquake waves, seismic waves, or shock waves. The waves cause the rock to expand and then compress as the energy moves through it.

Most earthquake damage is caused by waves on the surface of Earth, not underground.

Imagine holding a taut piece of rope tied to a doorknob in front of you. If you flick your wrist, a pulse, or wave, will travel through the rope similarly to the way in which a shock wave travels. You can easily see the up-and-down wave action. These vertical waves are called **transverse waves**. Not easily seen are **longitudinal waves**, which expand and compress the rope horizontally. It is easier to visualize longitudinal waves by thinking of snapping a rubber band. The elastic expands and compresses in the same way that rocks affected by shock waves do.

These shock waves travel from the focus of an earthquake to the epicenter. When they reach the surface, and are no longer bound by neighboring rock, their energy can cause severe damage.

What are P-waves and S-waves?

The shock waves that travel through Earth from an earthquake's focus, or point of origin, are known as P-waves and S-waves.

The P in P-waves stands for primary because they travel faster (about 15,000 mph, 24,000 kph) than S-waves, or secondary waves (about 10,000 mph, 16,000 kph). P-waves are longitudinal (horizontal), expanding and compressing rock. S-waves are transverse (vertical), moving up and down.

Why are P-waves and S-waves important?

P-waves and S-waves move through solids at different speeds from each other, and through different kinds of solids (such as granite and sandstone) at different speeds. Every seismographic station has a chart that gives the relationship between time and distance travel for each kind of wave, given the unique environment around the station. The difference in time between when the P- and S-waves registered on the seismographs is plotted on the chart. The chart then provides the distance the waves have traveled.

Let's say that three seismographic stations record the traveling distance of the same shock waves. A circle is drawn around each station at the distance recorded. The point at which the three circles intersect is the earthquake's epicenter.

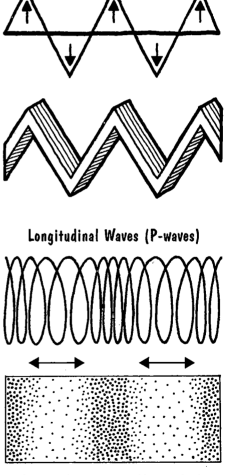

Transverse Waves (S-waves)

Longitudinal Waves (P-waves)

Underground transverse and longitudinal shock waves cause the surrounding rock to expand and compress during an earthquake.

Using the same specialized graph, scientists can tell exactly when the earthquake hit the epicenter. If the epicenter is 100 miles (160 kilometers) away and it takes P-waves 24 seconds to travel 100 miles (160 kilometers) to a specific seismograph, the earthquake hit the epicenter 24 seconds before the seismograph recorded the P-waves.

What kinds of surface waves are there?

Just as P-waves and S-waves move in horizontal and vertical directions, respectively, there are corresponding horizontal and vertical surface waves: Love waves and Rayleigh waves.

Love waves, named for the British mathematician A. E. H. Love, are waves on the surface that expand and compress particles horizontally along the path of the tremor.

Lord Rayleigh, a British physicist, described surface waves in which particles move vertically, perpendicularly to Love waves. These waves were named Rayleigh waves.

How do surface waves cause earthquake damage?

Love and Rayleigh waves travel more slowly than P- and S-waves, but they have larger horizontal and vertical movements. When the underground seismic waves reach the surface, they no longer have to travel through solid rock. Waves move more quickly on the surface because it is much less dense than solid rock and is surrounded primarily by air. This allows for much greater movement and much greater destruction.

Buildings built securely on bedrock have a better chance of surviving surface waves because bedrock is more difficult to move. If buildings are built on a softer foundation, the waves can shift the ground particles to a greater extent, causing more damage. Solidity is not

always the answer, however, because under enough stress, solids will snap. Buildings made of materials that can give, or withstand stress without breaking, may suffer less damage. Almost nothing, however, will last if it sits directly on top of an actual fault.

What else, besides shaking, happens during an earthquake?

Atmospheric pressure can change drastically during an earthquake. The force of released energy will simply push a mass of air pressure, temporarily dislocating it. In 1969, during an earthquake in Japan, the air 210 miles (336 kilometers) above Earth temporarily shot up about 1 mile (1.6 kilometers).

Spouts of sand, mud, steam, and water have all been seen shooting up during quakes. These geyserlike streams can reach higher than 20 feet (6 meters).

Earthquake effects can stimulate all of our senses. Not only will we feel the ground shake, but we might see a dome of earthquake light hanging over the ground—a result of released electricity and water vapor—or sheets of lightning. There may be smelly fumes—especially sulfur—coming from local water. The unpleasant taste of sulfur is sometimes in both the air and water. And, perhaps most frightening, we might hear great rumblings coming from within the earth.

What does an earthquake sound like?

Imagine hearing thunder, explosions, or cracking under the ground, or the roar of an underground train where there is no subway. All of these sounds may be heard during or even up to 2 weeks before an earthquake. The noise is the sound of earth actually moving and breaking. These noises travel better through solid ground than softer terrain, and, during an earthquake, sometimes it is difficult to distinguish them from the crashing of structures and buildings above ground.

How do earthquakes affect bodies of water?

It makes sense that water levels can rise and fall during an earthquake given that shifting can open up pockets in the earth or squeeze existing water up and out. Whole lakes and rivers may be drained or flood their banks. Water in wells, buildings, and fountains may turn yellow, red, or black, and have the foul smell and taste of sulfur. The same can happen in natural bodies of water.

The 1158 earthquake that hit London, England, caused the Thames River to dry up.

On April 1, 1946, the tsunami created by the Aleutian Islands earthquake in Alaska traveled 2,000 miles (3,200 kilometers) in 4 hours to the island of Hawaii. Waves that were 4 feet (1.2 meters) high in the ocean rose to 55 feet (17 meters) before hitting the resort town of Hilo. The town was destroyed and 173 people died.

During the severely destructive Chilean earthquake of 1835, an entire harbor turned black.

A significant accompaniment to earthquakes, especially those that occur under oceans, are tsunamis, or seismic sea waves. Out in the ocean, these waves can go unnoticed. They may be hundreds of miles (kilometers) long, but generally they are no higher than 3 or 4 feet (1 to 1.2 meters). When tsunamis reach land, however, they become extremely destructive forces.

How do tsunamis cause great damage?

Out in the middle of the ocean, tsunamis, fast-moving waves resulting from an earthquake, are generally mild, reaching heights of about 3 or 4 feet (1 to 1.2 meters). As the ocean waves approach the shallower water of the shore, the rising sediment rapidly slows them down from about 600 to 100 miles per hour (960 to 160 kilometers). The force of the incoming waves creates a wall of water that may extend 200 feet (61 meters) high. As the wall crests and crashes along the coast, houses, public buildings, and great ships can be splintered like matchsticks or carried miles ashore. Streams and rivers leading inland cannot hold the massive influx of water and flood their banks.

How does rock physically adjust to strain?

The force of Earth's movement builds up in rock until it reaches its breaking point, creating a fracture. Stress acts upon the rock in four different ways, causing the rock to change its shape and size. **Tension**, when strain pulls rock in opposite directions, causes a rock to stretch, or flatten out. **Compression** is the reverse of that, when strain comes at the rock from opposite directions. This elongates a rock vertically. When the stress hits the rock from all directions it is called **uniform stress**. The rock then shrinks in size as its particles are squeezed together. When the rock is compressed from different angles, instead of head-on, the rock will shift diagonally, causing shear stress.

Do rock formations change as internal stress builds up?

Stressed rock goes through stages of change as the energy within builds up. In the first stage, **elastic deformation**, the rock will go back to its original shape once the stress is released.

If the stress reaches the rock's **elastic limit**, or the point where it can't go back to its original shape, the rock will be permanently deformed. This stage of stress is called **ductile deforma-tion**. Ductile deformation tends to bend layered rock into folds: **syncline**, or U-shaped; **anticline**, or bridge-shaped; **mono-cline**, which looks a little like an escalator; or **recumbent**, when the fold bends back on itself. Recumbent folds look something like toothpaste lying on a toothbrush in advertisements.

Anticline Fold

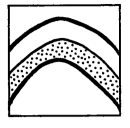

Syncline Fold

Monocline Fold

Recumbent Fold

Sometimes rock subjected to great pressure does not crack, but bends to form shapes called folds. Different types of folds are shown here.

Rock enters the final stage, **fracture**, when it is no longer able to bear the stress, and cracks. Fractured rock leads to faults and earthquakes.

Can we predict earthquakes?

People have been predicting earthquakes by watching natural phenomena for thousands of years. Accurate predictions, however, could only be made by people highly sensitive to their natural surroundings.

Prior to an earthquake, the water level in wells or ponds sometimes changes, as does the amount of turbulence and the temperature in the water. Animals may act strangely before an earthquake. Land may rise several inches (centimeters) over time before an earthquake. Knowing the history of earthquakes in the area adds to predictability, because quakes generally follow a pattern.

Some scientists believe that earthquakes can be predicted as accurately as the weather. Nowadays, scientific instruments can measure changes in the electrical currents of Earth; the volume of rock near a fault; the level of water and land; the amount of radon gas escaping from Earth; Earth's magnetic field; and the mounting stress within rock—all factors in predicting earthquakes. Many countries, particularly Russia, Japan, and the United States, have accelerated their research into earthquake prediction in this century. The number of faults under scientific observation, however, is a small fraction of the tens of thousands of miles (kilometers) of land prone to earthquakes.

Can earthquakes be prevented?

Earthquakes are a force of nature. They exist in order to release the tension built up by the movement of tectonic plates—the bases of Earth's crust. Preventing earthquakes would cause unimaginable destruction if it were even possible. And it is not possible.

Regulating earthquakes, however, may prove to be beneficial to society without damaging the natural order of Earth. Scientists have discovered that injecting liquid into fault zones can trigger mild earthquake activity. In one study, researchers were able to turn earthquakes on and off like a lamp. Perhaps releasing Earth's energy regularly in relatively mild tremors would limit the possibility of larger, more destructive quakes. One problem with this plan is that injecting anything into an already unstable area can cause the very earthquakes it is meant to prevent.

w many oceans are on Earth? ◆ What is th
ference between an ocean and a sea? ◆ Wher
e Earth's oceans located geographically? ◆ Ho
l our contemporary oceans form? ◆ How much o
rth's surfa_ _s covered by water? ◆ How muc
ter is in t○ o   ar○ ○ d ○ is he ocean?
hat is the a○ age ○○○ ○○ ○○○n? ◆ Why i
e ocean blue? ◆ What does the ocean floor loo
e? ◆ What does a continental shelf look like?
hat is a continental slope like? ◆ What does
ntinental rise look like? ◆ What is an abyssal plai

How many oceans are on Earth?

Depending on how you count, there are one to five oceans on Earth. A look at a globe of the world will show that all the ocean water is connected. Tradition, however, has divided up this superocean into the Pacific, Atlantic, Arctic, Antarctic, and Indian oceans. Sometimes the Pacific Ocean is divided again into the North Pacific and South Pacific oceans, and the same is true for the Atlantic. On the other hand, sometimes the Arctic and Antarctic oceans are spoken of as part of the Atlantic and Atlantic, Pacific, and Indian oceans, respectively. This can lead to confusion, but since all the waters flow into each other it is difficult to consider them as having hard and fast boundaries. In fact, we commonly refer to "the ocean," meaning all the oceans together. And sometimes we use the word "sea" to mean ocean, but we will try not to do so here.

Where are Earth's oceans located geographically?

The Pacific Ocean resides between the west coast of the American continents and the continents of Australia and Asia. The Atlantic Ocean spreads from the east coast of the Americas to Europe and Africa. The Indian Ocean is bordered by Africa to the west, the Mideast and India to

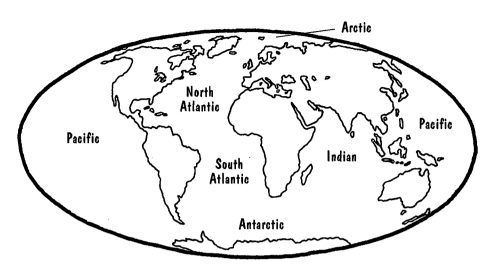

This map shows the Earth's oceans.

the north, and Indochina, Malaysia, Indonesia, and Australia to the east. The Arctic Ocean surrounds the Arctic, and the Antarctic Ocean surrounds Antarctica.

Seven Seas

Mariners have long used the phrase "seven seas" to describe the waters they sailed. Originally, they may have been referring to the Arabian Sea, the China Sea, the Indian Sea (ocean), the Mediterranean Sea, the Red Sea, the Persian Gulf, and the West African Sea (part of the Atlantic Ocean). In antiquity, however, the number seven was often used to mean many, uncountable, or all. Also, the word *sea* is commonly used in place of ocean. When used now, the phrase "seven seas" seems old-fashioned and suggests a romanticized view of life on the ocean.

How did our contemporary oceans form?

About 270 million years ago, the land that was to become the seven continents had formed Pangaea, one huge supercontinent. All around it flowed a superocean, called Panthalassa, or universal sea. Then, some 210 million years ago, Pangaea began to split up, creating a north-south rift that filled with water from Panthalassa. This waterway became the Atlantic Ocean. Land masses began floating to their current positions. More than 100 million years later, Pangaea had broken apart and between the moving continents, the Indian and Arctic oceans formed. By the time the continents had found their current locations, the Pacific and Antarctic oceans existed. At the same time the Atlantic Ocean was forming, water began to creep inland, creating seas and lakes.

How much of Earth's surface is covered by water?

An estimated 71 percent of Earth is covered by water. Only 29 percent of the surface is land. After viewing the world from space, one astronaut declared that there was so little land to be seen that our planet should be called "Water" instead of "Earth."

How much water is in the oceans?

The waters of all the oceans add up to an estimated 320,000 cubic miles (80,000 cubic kilometers). A cubic mile is one mile long, one mile wide, and one mile deep.

How deep is the ocean?

The answer depends on where you are taking the measurement. The floor of the ocean is similar to land surface in that it also has mountains and valleys, rock formations, vegetation, hills, trenches, and many other **topographical**, or surface, features.

Why is the ocean blue?

In fact, different oceans can appear to be different colors. At a distance, oceans may look blue; but, waves on a beach may appear greenish. Cold waters may appear a transparent green. Oceans may look gray, especially when stormy, or brownish near the shore if they are churning up sediment.

Objects absorb light from the Sun, which carries all the colors of the spectrum. They reflect back only certain colors depending on their physical makeup. A ripe tomato reflects red; a lemon reflects yellow. The waters of the ocean generally reflect blue.

In 1960, researchers took the deepest measurement of the ocean in history: just over 36,000 feet (11,000 meters) at the Marianas Trench in the Pacific Ocean.

World's Ten Deepest Ocean Trenches

Name	Ocean	Depth (miles/kilometers)	Width (mi./km.)	Length (mi./km.)
Marianas	West Pacific	6.8/11	43/69	1,600/2,560
Tonga	South Pacific	6.7/11	34/54	870/1,392
Kuril/Kamchatka (Russia)	North Pacific	6.5/10	74/118	1,400/2,240
Philippine	South Pacific	6.5/10	37/59	870/1,392
Japan	Pacific	5.2/8	62/99	500/800
Puerto Rico	Atlantic	5.2/8	74/118	960/1,536
South Sandwich (Falkland Islands)	South Atlantic	5.2/8	56/90	900/1,440
Peru/Chile	Pacific	5.0/8	62/99	3,700/5,920
Aleutian (Alaska)	North Pacific	4.8/7.7	31/50	2,300/3,680
Java (Indonesia)	Pacific	4.7/7.5	50/80	2,800/4,480

What does the ocean floor look like?

For many years, people thought the ocean floor was smooth and covered with silt or mud. Now, radar and sonar measurements, plus many explorations to the ocean floor, have revealed an amazing variety of structures. There are mountains (even higher than Mount Everest, the highest on Earth's surface), trenches, canyons, caves, rock formations, and virtually every other kind of topography, or natural structure, we see on land.

Five main components form the structure of the ocean floor. A **continental shelf** stretches out from land. This shelf is an extension of the continental plate, or land mass. It gradually declines, forming the **continental slope**, until it reaches the **continental rise**, the part of the ocean floor inclining to meet the slope. The floor then extends in an **abyssal plain** to the raised **ocean ridge**. Basically, one ocean ridge runs through the middle of the Atlantic, Arctic, Pacific, and Indian oceans. On the other side of the ridge is another abyssal plain reaching to another continental rise, another continental slope, and another continental shelf.

A continental shelf, slope, and rise are together known as a **continental margin**. The abyssal plains and ocean ridge make up the **ocean basin**.

What does a continental shelf look like?

Almost one sixth of Earth's surface is covered by continental shelves. They extend into the ocean from a land mass up to approximately 250 miles (400 kilometers), forming the shallow areas nearest the coast. The surface of a continental shelf tends to be smooth, though it rises and descends in hills and valleys. The shelf follows a gradual decline until abruptly dropping off at the end of the continental plate. There it meets the continental slope.

What is a continental slope like?

This steep slope connects the continental shelf to the continental rise. Usually about 60 miles (96 kilometers) long, the ocean floor here slopes rapidly at about a 4-degree angle, or 500 feet (152 meters) every mile (1.6 kilometers). The slope begins about a half mile (1 kilometer) below the ocean surface and plunges to almost 2 miles (3 kilometers) deep.

What does a continental rise look like?

Almost 2 miles (3 kilometers) deep, this part of the ocean floor gradually inclines, or rises, at a gentle 0.5-degree angle—less than a quarter the grade of the conti-

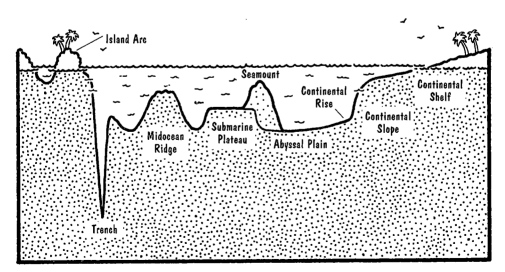

The ocean floor has many of the same features as dry land, including mountains, trenches, and plains.

nental slope. The floor here is smooth, though rises have mountains, which do not break the surface, and canyons. Rises extend about 440 miles (704 kilometers) from shore.

What is an abyssal plain like?

This part of the ocean floor is more than 3 miles (5 kilometers) deep. A plain is a relatively flat expanse of ground. Abyssal plains are wide, flat areas of the ocean floor on either side of the midocean ridge. Sediment covers the floor of abyssal plains, deposited there by particle-filled underwater currents. The rock under the sediment actually has a variety of hills and depressions. The sediment simply fills in the irregularities, making it appear flat. Abyssal plains generally stretch for about 150 miles (240 kilometers) between a continental rise and the midocean ridge.

What is the midocean ridge?

The midocean ridge can be thought of as a 31,000-mile (49,600-kilometer) long mountain range that runs through the Atlantic, Arctic, Pacific, and Indian oceans. They resemble mountains on land with their ruggedness and surprising height. Points of the ridge can break through the water's surface. The island of Iceland

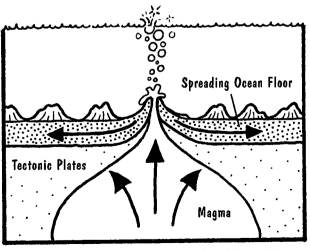

The underwater mountain range known as the midocean ridge marks where oceanic tectonic plates meet. There, magma constantly rises from beneath the ocean floor to re-create the mountains.

is, in fact, a part of the midocean ridge. Ocean research has shown that the midocean ridge is continually spreading out.

Rifts sometimes intersect this string of mountains like deep valleys. These rifts, or valleys, can dive deeper than 1 mile (1.6 kilometers) below sea level. There is evidence of a lot of volcanic and earthquake activity at the bottom of these valleys.

How does the midocean ridge grow?

Churning magma, or molten rock, from within Earth's mantle constantly rises up and breaks through the ridge. As the magma rises, it pushes the ridge horizontally in opposite directions, spreading it out. The magma cools to become a new part of the ridge. In this way, new ocean floor appears and pushes the older floor toward the continents.

If the ocean floor is spreading, why isn't it getting bigger?

The rifts, or trenches, that cut across the midocean ridge prevent the ocean floor from actually growing. The old ocean floor is dragged down into the trenches by the movement of the mantle, where it is destroyed by the process of **subduction**. Subduction occurs when a continental plate meets an ocean plate and the ocean plate is pushed under the continental plate. The part of the ocean plate that is pushed under winds up in Earth's mantle, where it melts into magma. This movement of plates is usually accompanied by earthquakes, which are common in ocean trenches. These earthquakes are most likely also responsible for the mountainous quality of the midocean ridge.

What are ocean trenches?

Trenches are long, deep, V-shaped indentations in the ocean floor where tectonic plates are subducting into the mantle. Trenches can be more than 6 miles (9.6 kilometers) deep and 3,500 miles (5,600 kilometers) long, but at the bottom most are only a mile or so wide. Sediment is usually found at the bottom of trenches, making their floors smooth. Heavy seismic, or earthquake, activity is also found down there.

What kinds of sediment are found on the ocean floor?

There are two basic types of ocean floor sediment. **Terrigenous sediment** washes off land into the ocean. **Pelagic sediment** is created within the ocean.

Terrigenous sediment finds its way into the ocean through rivers and streams, run-off from rainfall, winds, and glaciers. Quartz, feldspar, and clay mineral deposits common to terrestrial rock get into the ocean this way.

Pelagic sediment comes from many sources in the ocean. Decaying life forms supply sedimentary particles, especially creatures with shells of calcium carbonate, which is a compound found in chalk and limestone. Many microscopic creatures, such as phytoplankton, grow these shells. After death, the animals sink toward the ocean floor. These decaying animals with their calcium carbonate shells on the floor are called **calcareous oozes**. If the ocean floor is more than 16,500 feet (5,030 meters) deep, however, pressure disintegrates the shells and they dissolve into the water.

Some microscopic organisms grow silica shells. **Siliceous oozes** are the undissolved remains of these shells. Silicon is an abundant element found in quartz and flint. People use silicon in creating glass and ceramics.

What is ocean water made of?

Many people would answer this question by saying water and salt. They would be only partially correct. Pure water makes up 96.5 percent of ocean water. More sodium chloride, or common table salt, exists in ocean water than any other salt, but it is only one of many salts found there. Salts are a certain class of chemical compounds, or combinations, which generally form minerals. The other 3.5 percent of ocean water is made of dissolved minerals, **organic** matter, dissolved gases, and floating particles. Matter that comes from plants and animals is called organic.

The most commonly found minerals come from combinations of the elements chlorine, sodium, magnesium, sulfur, calcium, and potassium. They include dissolved carbon, carbohydrates, proteins, acids, and vitamins. Decaying plants and animals and fecal matter from living animals supply most of the organic matter.

What is salinity?

The percentage of dissolved salts, or salt minerals, present in a sample of water is called salinity. Salinity varies depending on how much salt has dissolved in the water—until the water reaches its saturation point, when it can contain no more salt. Factors that help determine the salinity of water include evaporation, precipitation, and land and ice run-off. Evaporation and land run-off increase water's salinity. Precipitation and melting ice reduce it.

What happens when the water cannot hold any more salt?

When water has reached the point where it cannot hold any more dissolved minerals, these minerals **precipitate out** of the water. This means that they separate from the water in a solid form again. The minerals then sink to the ocean floor. Saturation usually results from evaporation of the water. As the amount of pure water is reduced, the amount of minerals that remains is more than the water can hold.

Different minerals separate from water at different points. Calcite and dolomite precipitate out first, followed by gypsum. Halite, sodium chloride in rock crystal formation, then separates from the water. Magnesium and

The Great Salt Lake

The Great Salt Lake of Utah lies about 5 miles northwest of Salt Lake City. It is the largest salt lake on the North American continent at 72 miles (115 kilometers) long, 30 miles (48 kilometers) wide, and 27 feet (8 meters) deep. Some 300,000 tons (304,800 metric tons) of salt are extracted from it every year.

To the southwest of the Great Salt Lake, the Great Salt Lake Desert extends 140 by 80 miles (224 by 128 kilometers). Included in this desert are the Bonneville Salt Flats, vast stretches of hard, salt-encrusted land famous as a testing ground for race cars. This desert is a good location to see mirages on sweltering hot days.

The lake, desert, and flats were all once part of the vast prehistoric Lake Bonneville.

potassium are the last minerals to precipitate out of water—if the process gets that far.

If all the water evaporates, the minerals are left in **evaporite deposits**. The Mediterranean Sea is a good example of salt deposits underwater. Because the sea is almost completely landlocked, more water evaporates than enters. The seawater, therefore, has a high salinity rate and thick salt deposits on its floor.

What is the temperature of the ocean?

The temperature of the ocean can vary between below freezing, 32° Fahrenheit (0° Celsius), and just below vaporization, the point where liquid water becomes water vapor. Sunlight, atmospheric temperature, and condensation of water vapor all heat the surface of the water. The warmer surface generally remains separate from lower, colder water, unless winds or currents stir it up.

Volcanic activity can cause ocean water to boil and vaporize.

The surface is defined by how deep sunlight can penetrate. Sunlight reaches between about 300 and 1,600 feet (91 and 488 meters) into the water. Beneath the surface lies the **thermocline**, a region where temperatures drop sharply. In the thermocline, temperatures steadily decrease all the way down to the ocean floor.

Surface ocean water can remain liquid below 32° Fahrenheit (0° Celsius) because the salt content doesn't allow it to freeze. Subzero water near the ocean floor does not freeze because of the immense amount of pressure on it.

What kinds of animals live in the ocean?

Whole books are written about the huge variety of animal life in the ocean. Fish, mammals, crustaceans, microscopic organisms, reptiles, birds, and virtually every other kind of creature—with the exception of *Homo sapiens*—live in the ocean. In fact, the ocean is home to 95 percent of all life on the planet Earth.

Does ocean water circulate?

Wind is one major cause of ocean water circulation. **Surface currents** follow the pattern of wind above the ocean. Worldwide, winds near the equator blow from the east, causing currents to travel westward. When the surface currents approach land masses, they turn north or south in **deflected currents**. Deflected currents are very strong because they carry the force of water that has traveled all the way across the ocean uninterrupted. The winds about halfway between the equator and North and South Poles blow from the west—the opposite direction from equatorial winds. The currents again traverse the oceans until they reach land masses and are deflected back toward the equator. The whole route of these surface currents forms a circular pattern called a **gyre**. The Indian Ocean has a smaller gyre, because it is a smaller ocean.

The difference in water temperatures is another cause of water circulation far beneath the surface. Equatorial water is much warmer than polar water because the Sun heats the water at the equator more than at the North and South Poles. Because warm water floats on top of cold water, the colder water at the poles sinks below the

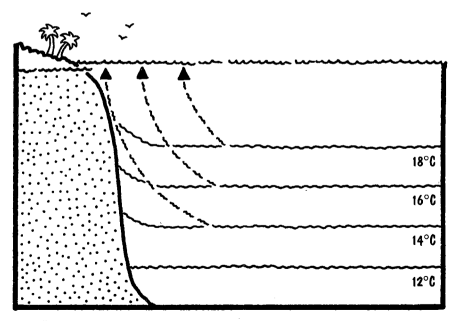

Upwelling occurs when warm, often nutrient-rich water rises to the surface.

warmer currents circulating from the equator. Deep in the ocean, the cold water flows back toward the equator, causing the warmer water there to rise. Warm water rising to the surface is called **upwelling**. Currents that result from the difference in temperatures are called **convection currents**.

The circulation of ocean water happens slowly. Surface currents take about 10 years to complete their cycle. Deep underwater currents travel from the poles to the equator and back in about 1,000 years.

What would happen if ocean water didn't circulate?

Convection currents circulate the enormous amount of heat stored in the ocean and churn up nutrients—such as nitrate, oxygen, and phosphate. If the cold water from the poles did not displace the warm equatorial water, the heat within Earth would raise the temperature of the ocean floor. Sooner or later, it would be hotter than the surface temperature. The upwelling of water from the bottom would release devastating quantities of carbon dioxide, destroying both marine and coastal life.

Are there storms under the ocean?

Abyssal storms have created drifts of sediment on the ocean floor 1 mile (1.6 kilometers) thick, 600 miles (960 kilometers) long, and 100 miles (160 kilometers) wide.

The motion from ocean currents causes storms, somewhat similar to the atmospheric ones we experience on the planet's surface. The currents that run along the shore can move at about 1 mile (1.6 kilometers) per hour. This has the same effect as 45-mile (72-kilometer)-per-hour winds along the coast, stirring up sediment and re-creating the ocean floor.

Just as air currents cause storms on the ocean surface midway between the equator and the poles, similar eddies, or whirlpools, occur underwater. The result of these storms, which can last for weeks, is a redistribution of sediment from the ocean floor.

How are waves created?

Wind creates the most common waves. These waves begin in the open ocean where the energy of the wind is transferred to the water. Energy, not water, is the driving

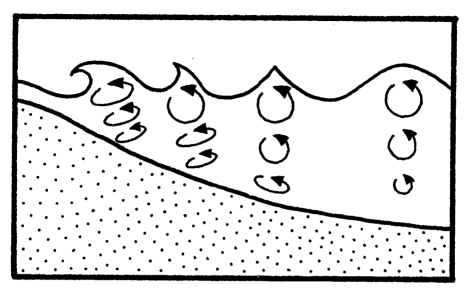

Wind blowing over water creates waves. Individual water particles do not move along with the wave. They move in a circle, as indicated in this drawing. Waves break at the shore because the water particles at the bottom of the wave are slowed down by the rising ocean floor, while the water particles at the top of the wave continue to move.

force behind waves. Picture a ball floating on the water at the beach. When a wave reaches it, the ball rides to the top of the wave and then down the wave's back side, ending up almost exactly where it began. Meanwhile, the wave continues on toward the shore. If water rather than energy were on the move, the ball would be carried ashore on the wave. Instead, we see energy passing through the water in the form of the wave.

Oceanologists—people who study oceans—have not yet completely figured out how this transfer of energy from the wind to the water takes place. They do know, however, that wind blowing over the ocean surface is deflected, or turned away, by the water. Air deflected by an object rises, drawing the object upward. This upward movement is called lift. Not only water, but bird and airplane wings respond to lift. Under stormy conditions, the wind pushes down on the water like a hand. Both of these actions cause waves.

While the wind's energy travels through the water, the water does not stay still. Particles in the water show how the water moves. Under a wave, energy sets the particles moving in circular patterns. As the energy decreases in deeper water, particles move in smaller circles until it becomes a gentle rocking motion at great depths. The motion disappears around 325 feet (100 meters) down.

Do volcanoes and earthquakes cause waves?

Volcanoes and earthquakes release an enormous amount of energy from within Earth. This energy is passed on into ocean water creating waves that can be quite destructive.

Tsunamis, waves caused by volcanoes and earthquakes, can travel hundreds and thousands of miles (kilometers) before reaching a land mass. Out in the ocean, they reach only a few feet (meters) high, but as they near land, they slow down and increase dramatically in size. Tsunamis can be 100 feet (30 meters) tall when they reach shore. Their force has been known to destroy entire towns.

What are tidal waves?

Most of us think tidal waves are the huge waves that result from earthquakes and storms, but they really only refer to the water's movement during tides. Tides are the effect of the Moon's gravitational force. The water nearest the Moon, as it orbits Earth, bulges toward it. The precise term for the immense, destructive waves caused by earthquakes and storms is tsunamis.

How high can waves grow?

The height of a wave is measured from the crest, or top, to the trough, the point where the wave rises from the surface. A wave's height depends on the speed of the wind and the length of time the wind blows. The faster and longer the wind blows, the higher the waves will be. Unless whipped up by storms, midocean waves tend to be moderate, from a few feet to 15 feet (4.6 meters) high. (In the middle of the ocean, 15 feet is not considered big.) Waves can be minute ripples or they can be tsunamis, taller than trees and buildings.

How is wavelength measured?

Wavelength, the distance between waves, is measured from the crest of one wave to the crest of the next wave. Wavelengths up to 3,000 feet (914 meters) have been measured in the Pacific Ocean, though 1,000 feet (304 meters) is more common. Storm waves tend to have shorter wavelengths, 300 to 800 feet (91 to 244 meters).

What is a wave period?

Waves' speed, or **period**, is measured by clocking how fast a complete wave crosses a designated point. Fast wave periods result from strong, long-blowing winds. Out in the ocean, wave periods range from less than one tenth of a second to more than 24 hours. Depending on their speed, most waves are classified as **gravity waves** (greater than one tenth of a second and less than 5 minutes) or **long waves** (more than 5 minutes, but less than 12 hours). Along the coastline, most wind-generated waves have periods between 5 and 20 seconds.

What is a wave fetch?

Wave fetch designates the area in an ocean over which wind is blowing at a given time. Fetch is a factor in determining wave height, period, and wavelength. In a large fetch, wavelengths will be greater. In a small fetch, waves will be closer together.

What are wave swells?

Swells define waves that move uniformly after leaving a fetch, or the area in which they were created. Swells are symmetrically shaped. The farther they travel, the lower they get, but their horizontal length remains constant. If swells do not encounter a land mass or other obstacle, they can travel clear across the ocean.

Why do waves break on the shore?

By the time waves reach the shore, the water itself is moving, not just the energy traveling through it. Breaking waves, or **surf**, occurs when the wave reaches water of a depth equal to or less than one half of its wavelength, the distance between waves. The land slows down the water

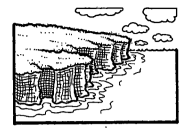

at the bottom of the wave, causing the faster upper part, the **crest** of the wave, to rise and arc, finally crashing down on itself. The crest breaks because it outraces the lower part of the wave and winds up hanging in the air. Gravity draws it back down.

How does the ocean affect the coastline?

Where the ocean meets land, a variety of coastlines are created through the process of erosion. Many factors dictate the specific characteristics of each coastline—whether cliffs, beaches, or estuaries—including current or wave action and geologic components of the land.

How are cliffs made?

Cliffs result when heavy wave activity eats away at a hard slope of land. Depending on the hardness of the cliff rock and the angle of the rock layers, a cliff may be a gentle slope down to the ocean or a dramatic steep drop or overhang. If the layers of the cliff's rock tilt upward as they reach the coastline, the former will most likely occur. If the layers tilt down toward the water, however, the waves will eat away at the base of the cliff, creating an indentation. Sooner or later, once the waves erode enough rock at the base of the cliff, the rest of the cliff will fall into the ocean.

Does ocean water ever flood coastal rivers?

Some of the most dramatic coastlines occur when the ocean flows into mountainous river valleys. One example, **Dalmatian coastlines**, are named for the coast of Dalmatia, on the Adriatic Sea. There, the water flooded mountain valleys parallel to the coastline, creating inland **sounds**, or long inlets of water, running in the same direction as the coastline. **Rias**, which can be found in southwest England, are flooded valleys that run perpendicular to the coast.

The ocean can also infiltrate low-lying riverbeds. An **estuary** is a flooded river mouth on a mud plain. At low tides the ocean water recedes to uncover many creeks and little islands of mud. While fjords are steep water-filled valleys created by glaciers in highlands, **fjards** are lowland ocean inlets created by glaciers and studded with small islands. Southern Sweden has many fjards.

What are beaches?

Most of us think of long stretches of sun-drenched sand when we hear the word *beach*, but a variety of shorelines make up beaches. Sand beaches are one kind of beach, but the term includes just about any low-lying shore formation and material. Boulder beaches, sand beaches, bay-head beaches, dune beaches, sand bars, spits, and mud flats all qualify.

What are boulder beaches?

Just as the term implies, boulder beaches are low shorelines filled with rocks and boulders at the base of cliffs. The rocks and boulders result from wind and weather erosion or water erosion that knocks down chunks of the cliff. The ocean will further erode the pebbles and rocks, eventually turning them into grains of sand.

How are sand beaches and sand bars formed?

Sand beaches are made of sediment from the ocean and from land. What the sediment is made of depends on what is available from the surrounding environment. Wave activity carries the sediment between the ocean and the beach. Strong, quick waves do not give the particles of sediment time to settle on the floor. They stay in motion, dragged farther from land until they reach calmer water. There the sediment settles to the bottom, often creating sand bars or barriers.

Calmer waves deposit sediment on the shore. Much of it is swept back toward the ocean, but enough time passes before the next wave to allow the sediment to settle. As a result, more sediment builds up along the shore.

What are dune beaches?

Simply put, dune beaches are beaches with **dunes** on them. Mountains of shifting sand are called dunes. Wind will kick up grains of sand on the beach and as the grains fall back to Earth, they dislodge more sand, and on and on. When the moving mass of sand meets an obstacle—a plant, tree, or fence—it can go no further. The wind does not stop, however, so the sand forms a slope against the barrier. As the wind continues, sand is blown up the slope and over the top, or crest. Suddenly it is sheltered from the wind by the slope it just surmounted, so it falls, ultimately creating another slope on the other side. As the process of sand blowing over the top doesn't stop, the mountain of sand, or dune, gradually progresses over the land.

What are spits?

A spit is a bar of sand or other sediment that is still connected at one end to the mainland. The sand is deposited by waves, currents, and tides. Barrier spits are actually bars that cut off a small part of water inland; the body of water becomes a lagoon. Double spits look like barrier spits except that they do not completely meet as they come out from shore. They don't actually cut off water to form a lagoon. Tombolos are spits that connect the mainland to an island. Cape Canaveral, Florida, the site of many rocket launches, is actually a triangular spit of sediment called a cuspate foreland.

hat is the difference between ocean water an
eshwater? ◆ How much fresh water is there?
hat is the difference between rivers an
eams? ◆ What is the longest river in the world
How streams and rivers erode the land? ◆ D

FRESHWATER

ean streams and rivers always run in the sam
ection? ◆ How do lakes form? ◆ What is th
gest lake on the face of Earth? ◆ Why are th
rth American Great Lakes so great? ◆ How d

What is the difference between ocean water and freshwater?

Freshwater does not contain a substantial amount of salt. Streams and rivers generally carry freshwater on land. Inland seas and lakes can be either fresh- or saltwater, depending on the source of the water. Freshwater comes from precipitation—rain and melted snow—whereas saltwater comes from the ocean.

How much freshwater is there?

About 1 percent of all water on Earth is freshwater from lakes, streams, and ponds. As ocean water evaporates, however, it leaves behind most of its salt content and becomes pure water vapor in the atmosphere. Then again, since 71 percent of Earth is covered by ocean, most precipitation falls back into the ocean and becomes saltwater again, so it doesn't affect the amount of freshwater.

What is the difference between rivers and streams?

Stream is the word used for a channel of flowing water. A river is a large stream.

Streams originate in high ground, though the slope is not always noticeable with the naked eye. They can be fed by a number of sources. Rain and melting snow and glaciers can feed streams. Some streams run out of lakes. Streams can also be formed by shifting earth releasing underground water.

When the ground becomes saturated (cannot hold any more water), the water gathers on the surface and the force of gravity channels it through the terrain in a stream. Depending on the hardness and density of the land, the stream develops quickly or slowly. Rivers are

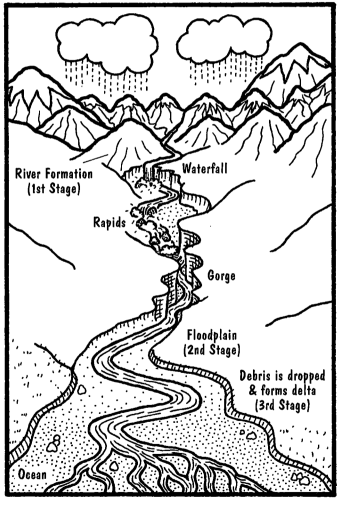

From high ground to low, rivers erode and change the landscape. Stages 1, 2, and 3 represent youth, adulthood, and old age in a river, as well as its progress to the sea.

fed by smaller streams. They barrel through the terrain, ultimately carrying water and sediment to the ocean. Inevitably, however, the eroding, or wearing away, force of running water cuts through the earth. Because gravity forces everything down to the lowest point, rivers continue until they reach the ocean, the lowest level of land—sea level.

What is the longest river in the world?

At 4,180 miles (6,688 kilometers) long, the ancient and famous Nile River in Africa can lay claim to the title of longest river. The Nile flows from Lake Victoria, on the equator, and twists and turns (an indication of its old age) to its **mouth**, or outlet, on the Mediterranean Sea.

Some experts claim that the Amazon River in South America is actually longer than the Nile. The difference of opinion stems from how the river's distance is measured. If you take into account all the interconnecting **tributaries**, or side rivers, the Amazon is the longest.

How do streams and rivers erode the land?

Streams and rivers cause erosion in two ways. The force of running water cuts a channel into the earth, sometimes forming valleys or steep gorges. Then, running water picks up sediment—particles of earth called **silt**—and carries it away from its original spot. When a stream has cut a path through the land, it creates a new destination for run-off from the surrounding terrain. Streams and rivers transport silt from their origin and gather more along their journey toward the ocean.

A new stream will form a relatively steep, V-shaped channel in the earth. It may contain waterfalls and rapids. Over time, with more and more running water, the channel will smooth out and become a gentler, wider U shape. The stream will create a **floodplain**, a low-lying area that is subject to flooding when the stream overflows, with the actual water flow running in a channel through it. As streams age, they tend to wander, or meander, in loops through their floodplain. A stream can be identified as old by the presence of extensive meandering.

When the stream reaches the ocean, it may form a **delta**. A delta is a fan-shaped deposit of silt from the river. Deltas result from the running water dropping its **load**—the silt it is carrying—into the ocean. The load is dropped because the stream's water slows when it reaches the larger ocean, allowing gravity to force the silt to settle.

Over time streams have been known to wash away entire mountains.

Do streams and rivers carry a lot of silt?

The quantity of silt, or sediment, a stream or river can transport is called its **capacity**. The amount it carries at any given point in time is its load. The estimated depth of erosion from streams is less than half an inch (one centimeter) every 300 years.

What is sheetwash?

When rain, or other precipitation, falls on already saturated land, it washes over the surface in sheets before coming together in rivulets. The rivulets then merge until they join streams. In some areas, sheetwash will find its way directly into lakes or rivers without first forming rivulets.

Do streams and rivers always run in the same direction?

No. Streams flow from high ground to low ground, but that is not always the same direction. Since the ultimate end for the rivers is the nearest ocean, however, the overall direction for rivers in the same area tends to be the same.

A **divide** is a ridge of high land that separates rivers flowing one direction from rivers flowing another. A **continental divide** works on a grand, continental scale. For instance, the continental divide in the United States is in the Rocky Mountains, separating eastward-flowing rivers from westward-flowing ones.

How do lakes form?

Precipitation on saturated land, especially land formed into a depression, will form a pond or lake. Lakes can also get their start from released water vapor and earth movements during a volcano or earthquake, plus precipitation. If a river meets a barrier, either a natural dam or a fabricated one, a lake will result from the buildup of water. Underground water may rise to the surface through land shifts, erosion, or springs to make a lake. Saltwater lakes can also be created by land cutting off a part of the ocean. Essentially, wherever water gathers without an outlet, a pond or lake will form.

What is the largest lake on the face of Earth?

The surface of Lake Superior, one of the five Great Lakes on the North American continent, measures 31,820 square miles (82,435 square kilometers). Its length alone is 383 miles (613 kilometers). Lake Superior has the largest surface of any lake on Earth, but it does not hold the most water.

Lake Baikal, which sits on a major fault in southeastern Siberia, contains one fifth of the total amount of freshwater on Earth, about 5,500 cubic miles (1,375 cubic kilometers) of water. Its surface area is easily one fourth or less than that of Lake Superior, but Lake Baikal is 5,712 feet (1,741 meters)—more than a mile (1.7 kilometers)—deep.

More than 300 rivers feed Lake Baikal in Russia.

Lake Baikal claims to be the oldest lake in the world, too. Some 80 million years ago, the fault shifted, creating a depression, or graben. Then, 25 million years ago, it began to fill with water.

Why are the North American Great Lakes so great?

These five lakes—Superior, Michigan, Huron, Erie, and Ontario—are actually the remnants of a once-greater prehistoric lake called Lake Algonquin. Together the Great Lakes hold about 20 percent of the world's freshwater. On the border of Canada and the United States, they are connected to each other and to the Atlantic Ocean by many rivers, canals, and the St. Lawrence Seaway, which allows major shipping to enter the continent's interior. Their combined surface area is more than 95,000 square miles (246,611 square kilometers).

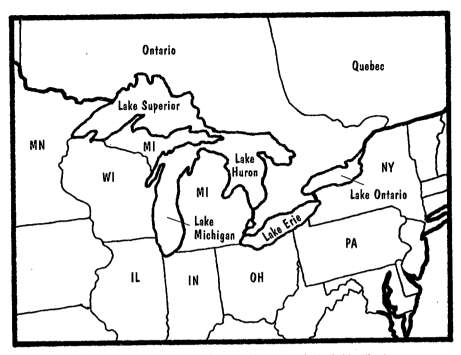

The five Great Lakes border Canada and the United States. Lake Baikal in Siberia, a very deep lake, contains about the same amount of water as all of the Great Lakes combined, but it has only about one eighth of their surface area.

This great size sometimes makes them act more like small oceans than lakes, with obvious tides, huge storms, currents, and accompanying shipwrecks.

How do lakes change over time?

Most lakes are fated to disappear over time. They can fill up with silt from the surrounding environment through rainfall, wind, or river deposits. Because water is always seeking a lower base, lakes may be drained by water seeping into the land. Great geological events can make lakes disappear, such as the destruction of a huge ice dam in Montana 15,000 years ago. Once the ice dam broke, the waters of the great Lake Missoula flooded the land and made its way to the ocean. Lakes may dry up through decreased precipitation and increased evaporation. The formation of new rivers can channel lake water away from its basin.

The destruction of lakes is not as dire as it sounds, however, because new lakes can be formed just as well. Almost everything that destroys a lake can also create one. Silt deposits can dam up rivers to form lakes. Drained lake water can form underground lakes or reemerge miles away. Geological activity creates lakes by filling up volcanic craters with water, or creating basins through earthquakes that are later filled by rain, groundwater, or melting glaciers. If the rate of precipitation outstrips evaporation, a lake may form. And rivers can run into obstacles that prevent them from continuing, so they pool up into lakes.

What are wetlands?

Wetlands are areas that contain a lot of water but are not ponds or lakes. Vanishing lakes as well as lakes in the process of forming can saturate the land for a time, creating distinct environments: marshes, swamps, and bogs.

Waterlogged land with an inch or two (2 to 4 centimeters) of standing water during flooding or heavy rain is called a marsh. Swamps are marshes that are always covered with water, sometimes a foot or two (30 to 60 centimeters) deep.

Areas of shallow ponds and pools covered with moss and other vegetation are called bogs. Bog water is often too acidic to support common wetland vegetation. Instead, you can find carnivorous plants, such as Venus's-flytraps and pitcher plants, growing in bogs. Or you could find less deadly plants, such as cranberries.

Some bog surfaces can support a lot of weight—even that of a person or tree; walking across such a bog, called a "quaking bog," is like walking on a waterbed.

What is overturn in lakes and ponds?

With the onset of cool weather in autumn, the temperature of lake and pond surface water decreases. When water cools, its particles contract, making it denser. Dense water sinks to the bottom bringing the warmer water to the surface. This process, known as **overturn**, provides circulation which distributes nutrients and prevents the water from becoming stagnant.

Why does ice float?

Most liquids become heavier when they solidify. Water, however, becomes lighter when it freezes. Its point of highest density is about 39° Fahrenheit (4° Celsius), which is 7° Fahrenheit (-14° Celsius) above freezing. Therefore, ice weighs less than water and floats.

If ice didn't float, it would sink to the bottom of the lake or pond. Even in warm months, the Sun would not be able to melt it through the surface water, so more and more ice would form. Over time, a pond or lake would become a solid mass of ice with just a few inches of water on top. Nothing could live in it.

How are waterfalls created?

Waterfalls usually occur in young rivers, which haven't had enough time to wear down all the land in its path. Rushing water erodes softer materials before harder ones. Where the terrain includes both soft and hard materials, the water carries away the soft material, but must fall over the harder material. Cliffs of hard rock take the longest time to erode, so water winds up cascading— sometimes great lengths—over them to continue its path.

At 3,281 feet (1,000 meters), Angel Falls in Venezuela holds the record as the highest waterfall in the world. Niagara Falls, between Canada and the United States, is only 167 feet (51 meters) high. But these dramatic falls stretch over 1,060 feet (323 meters) of land and 1.25 million gallons (5.6 million liters) of water rushes over them every second. As with all waterfalls, Niagara Falls is moving upstream as the water continues to erode the land.

What are rapids?

Rapids occur in a fast-moving stream littered with large, hard rock formations. Water erodes soft land faster than hard, so the rocks remain standing as incomplete barriers. The stream's fast-moving water rushes around the rocks, often foaming into "white water." The flow of water is split into various streams and then reconnects as it rounds the rocks. Old rivers do not usually have rapids since, over time, their rushing water has eroded any barriers.

Is there water underground?

People depend largely on underground freshwater for personal use, agriculture, and industry. Rivers and lakes occur underground, and water is also retained inside rocks, dirt, and other materials that make up Earth's crust.

How do rivers and lakes exist underground?

Rivers run underground for the same reasons, and as a result of the same causes, as rivers on the surface. Earth's crust soaks up precipitation until it can hold no more. Some areas of the crust are so absorbent that water gathers deep underground. If the crust's material is more easily eroded underground, the water will begin to flow under the surface. It may emerge onto the surface at a later point in its course if the terrain changes. In the same way, a surface river can disappear underground if the rock material is more easily eroded there.

Similarly, underground lakes have the same characteristics as surface lakes. Whether water gathers above ground or underground depends on the ability of the surrounding environment to absorb water. Precipitation falling on saturated ground might erode the softer earth underground until it reaches a resilient layer instead of pooling on the surface.

How do rocks hold water?

The ability of rock to hold water depends on its **porousness**, or the number of pores—spaces—in the rock that water can get into. If a rock's pores are connected so that the water can circulate and be released, the rock is **permeable**. An underground area or layer of porous and permeable rock, from which we can extract water, is called an **aquifer**. The water held by rocks is known as **groundwater**.

What is the water table?

The water table is the boundary between an **unsaturated zone** and **saturated zone** underground. Because different materials absorb water to a greater or lesser extent, some layers of the crust can be filled with water

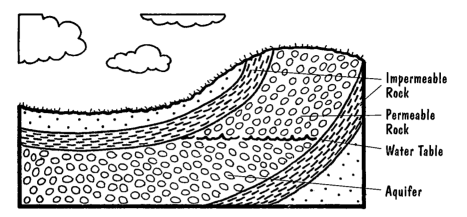

A layer of porous rock, the aquifer, holds groundwater between two layers of impermeable rock. Rain falling on the surface seeps down to add to the groundwater. The level of water in the aquifer is called the water table.

while other, even higher, levels are not filled at all or are only partially filled. The saturated zone refers to a layer of rock whose pores are full of water. Pores in the unsaturated zone are empty, or partially filled. The water table figuratively separates the two zones.

Knowing the depth of the water table in any given area helps when deciding what plants, crops, or trees to grow; how far you might have to dig a well to reach a constant supply of water; or whether a building will have a solid foundation.

What is the water cycle?

Most of our water came as a result of Earth's cooling after its creation. While new water is still formed on a small scale, we basically use the same water over and over again. The water cycle, also known as the hydrological cycle, is Earth's natural system for recycling water.

As a result of heat from the Sun, ocean water evaporates. Evaporation causes the pure liquid water (most of its salts remain on Earth) to expand and turn into vapor, or gas. The expanded molecules cool as the vapor rises into the atmosphere. The change in temperature causes

Fish Rain

History abounds with tales of small animals falling from the sky during rainstorms. A Greek author wrote of raining fish in the second century A.D. Fish falling from the sky have been reported throughout the centuries in India, Scotland, England, and the United States. Herring, catfish, perch, trout, bass, and shad have all been reported as raining from the sky. Tadpoles frequently appear in the fish rain reports, and frogs are not uncommon.

The phenomenon has been so widespread that many scientists have struggled to come up with a good theory to cover it. For a time, people believed a huge floating ocean existed in the atmosphere. Sometimes it leaked. Others never believed in the truth of the stories to begin with. In 1921, a scientist by the name of E. W. Gudger published a collection of these stories in a nature magazine along with possible explanations for the phenomenon. Gudger came up with a plausible theory: Whirlwinds and waterspouts can suck incredible amounts of water and the contents of whole ponds into the air. If the whirlwinds travel some distance before calming down, the fish would be carried by the more than 100-mile (160-kilo-meter)-an-hour winds until the force of the winds abated and gravity made the fish fall from the sky.

the vapor to condense back into liquid, in the form of tiny droplets. These droplets combine until they become too large to remain suspended in the air. They fall back to Earth as rain, snow, or other forms of precipitation. Where the precipitation falls back onto the ocean, the process immediately begins again.

Not all rain or snow falls back into the ocean, however. A small amount will evaporate from the surface of Earth again. Some will fall into lakes or rivers that ultimately find their way back to the ocean. Still other amounts of precipitation will become groundwater, either gradually combining with streams headed toward the ocean or going through a longer process—as drinking water, irrigation, or water in a car wash, for example. Sooner or later, though, all water makes its way back to the air through evaporation.

About 3 trillion tons (2.7 million metric tons) of ocean water evaporate a day.

The water cycle is a continous process. Air absorbs water from oceans, lakes, and rivers. Air also absorbs the water vapor exhaled by plants and animals. When the air rises, it cools, and the water vapor condenses to form a cloud. As soon as the cloud becomes too heavy with liquifying vapor, precipitation sends the water back to Earth.

How long does it take for water to be recycled through evaporation and precipitation?

Although water can be reused almost infinitely, any one drop may go through a long process before it is available again. It might sink into the ground and remain there for half a century. Or the drop might freeze into a snowflake and fall on a glacier in the Alps, where it could stay for thousands of years.

On the other hand, water that evaporated yesterday over the Pacific Ocean might become tomorrow's storm. A drop might fall right back into the ocean and evaporate again the following day.

If the water cycle purifies water, why is pollution a problem?

Most minerals are left behind when water evaporates, making rain freshwater rather than saltwater. This makes rainwater relatively pure, but atmospheric and surface pollution can reverse the process.

The burning of fossil fuels, such as coal, injects sulfur dioxide into the atmosphere. Nitrous oxide from automobile exhaust lingers in the air, too. When sulfur dioxide and nitrous oxide combine with humidity—evaporated water from the ocean, for instance—they create two very destructive acids: sulfuric acid and nitric acid. The once-pure rain that falls back to Earth contains these acids, which can kill life and destroy Earth's crust. The common name for this is **acid rain**.

Not only does acid rain hurt the environment, but when polluted water first evaporates, it leaves behind impurities (just as ocean water leaves salt behind). Those impurities follow their own cycle of sorts, seeping into groundwater and traveling in rivers to the ocean, where the water evaporates again, leaving toxic remains to further pollute the water supply.

hat is the difference between weather an
mate? ◆ Is climate more important than weather
What determines climate? ◆ What is latitude?
hat is longitude? ◆ What does latitude have to d
th clim te? ◆ What consequences does the ai
ve on te na d er es th
mperatur of the ai ? What is o one? ◆ Wha
the ozone hole? ◆ What is the greenhous
fect? ◆ What does deforestation have to do wit
e greenhouse effect? ◆ How can Earth survive i
is so delicately balanced? ◆ What is air pressure

WEATHER

What is the difference between weather and climate?

We all know what weather is. It's what we look out the window to check before going outside every day. Do I need an umbrella? Where are my boots? I need sunblock. I'd better wear a hat. Translated into weather terms, you are checking on rain, snow, sunshine, and wind, just some of the manifestations, or types, of weather. Climate averages and generalizes the day-to-day weather of a specific area over a long period of time to broadly describe its weather patterns. Climate is the big picture, concerned with generalities. Arid, polar, temperate, subtropical—these are some of the adjectives used to describe climate.

Climatology, the study of climate, helps us understand the different environments on Earth: what happens to water; how do winds blow; are the polar ice caps likely to melt? Studying weather can help you predict what's happening in your environment: is that hurricane off the coast likely to hit our town; will this drought last another week; can our city afford to pay for plowing this snow?

What determines climate?

The basics of climate are temperature and moisture. To arrive at an overall view of these, however, scientists consider various factors, including latitude (north-south location on Earth), air, winds, clouds, and storm fronts.

What is latitude?

Scientists, geographers, and navigators, among others, use an imaginary grid laid on top of Earth to pinpoint a specific geographic area. You can see the horizontal lines (latitudes) and vertical lines (longitudes) on almost all maps and globes. Latitude measures points north and south; longitude measures points east and west.

Latitudes measure the angular distance of a point between the North or South Pole and the equator. Imagine bisecting Earth at the equator. One arm of your angle reaches out from the center of Earth to the equator. The other arm of the angle can point to any other place on Earth—the equator is a 0° angle and the geographic North and South Poles are 90° angles. Take New York City, for example. The three points of your angle would be on the center of Earth, the equator, and New York City, respectively. The measure of the angle is 40°. New York City is, therefore, 40° north latitude.

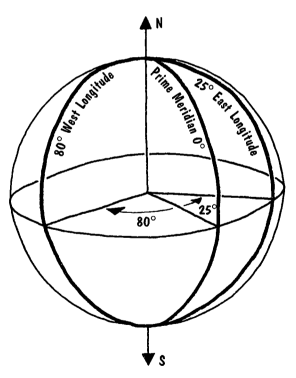

What is longitude?

Longitude divides Earth between east and west. Instead of bisecting the world horizontally at the equator, we draw an imaginary line from the North and South Poles called the **prime meridian**, which travels through Greenwich, England. The prime meridian is 0° longitude. (On the opposite side of the globe from the prime meridian is 180° longitude. The international

This drawing shows how longitude is determined. Exactly opposite the prime meridian (0° longitude) is 180° longitude. The longitude of a particular place is given as a point between 0° and 180° east or west of the prime meridian.

The longitudinal angle of New York City is 74° west, making the latitudinal and longitudinal coordinates for New York City 40° north and 74° west.

date line roughly follows this longitude.) Of the three points that determine the longitudinal angle, one is on the prime meridian, one on the imaginary line through Earth between the North and South Poles, and one is the point on the surface whose longitude you want to discover.

What does latitude have to do with climate?

Latitude helps determine the temperature of a locale. Since one of the most important factors of climate is the amount of energy, or radiation, received from the Sun (heat), latitude plays a critical role.

Climatologists (people who study climate) use the word **insolation** for energy that reaches Earth from the Sun. The word combines syllables from the phrase **in**coming **sol**ar radi**ation**. Sunlight is the obvious sign of insolation, but the Sun's radiation reaches the earth on a cloudy day too. The angle and duration of insolation, which translates into surface temperature, changes depending on latitude.

Because Earth is spherical, when it orbits the Sun, the Sun's rays hit Earth's surface directly at the equator and at angles near the poles. Direct insolation is stronger than slanted contact.

Earth also tilts on its axis, so when the Southern Hemisphere is closer to the Sun, it has more hours of daylight than the Northern Hemisphere, and vice versa. At the equator, the hours of night and day remain 12 hours each. But most of us have experienced the shorter days of winter and the longer days of summer that come from Earth rotating at a tilt.

Latitudes that receive direct insolation for many hours a day tend to have warmer climates, such as at the equator. Latitudes toward the North and South Poles get angled insolation for fewer hours overall, and have colder climates.

What determines the temperature of the air?

The temperature of the surface primarily determines the temperature of the air above it. Objects in the air, such as clouds or smoke and dust particles—either natural or produced—affect the air temperature. The air can receive heat reflected off clouds or particles just as it absorbs it from Earth's surface.

Water absorbs more heat than land, but gives off less of what it absorbs than land does. On a sunny day, then, air above a shoreline warms more quickly over the land than over the water. When the Sun sets, however, the water has retained more heat and so the air over the water can be warmer than the air over the land.

Atmospheric heat is caused by the speeding up of molecular movement in the air. The air is made of many **molecules** moving around independent of each other. When heat from the surface reaches them, they begin to move more quickly. Cold makes them slow down.

Earth's surface heats the air above it; if the ground or water is well-heated, the air will be warm.

What is ozone?

A unique form of oxygen, known as ozone, lies several miles (kilometers) above Earth in the atmosphere. It serves as a filter against the Sun's powerful and dangerous ultraviolet rays. Without this layer of atmospheric protection, ultraviolet radiation would cause many health problems, from skin irritation to cancer in humans, not to mention the harmful effects on other living creatures.

What is the ozone hole?

Ultraviolet radiation causes many health problems, including cancer. A layer of ozone in the atmosphere protects living things from ultraviolet radiation. A break, or hole, in the ozone layer exists over the southern polar region of Earth. This hole allows ultraviolet light from the Sun to reach Earth undiluted by ozone. Some scientists and environmentalists claim that this hole is growing as a result of pollution. It has only been recently studied, however, so others believe its expansion is probably a natural event.

The hole in the ozone is over a barren region of Earth, but imagine if it were to grow so large as to cover populated areas.

What is the greenhouse effect?

Natural gases in Earth's atmosphere create an environment similar to that found in the air of a greenhouse, specially designed for plant growth. In Earth's atmosphere,

greenhouse gases—carbon dioxide, methane, and nitrous oxide—allow the passage of the Sun's rays to Earth, which provides energy and heat. The gases make up only 0.03 percent of the atmosphere, but they prevent 30 percent of the heat rebounding from Earth's surface to escape back into space. While this keeps Earth warm enough for life, increasing the amount of these gases will increase the global temperature.

Industry and technology in the twentieth century have loaded the atmosphere with greenhouse gases, particularly carbon dioxide, which has increased 26 percent. In addition, the development of chlorofluorocarbons (CFCs) in the 1930s, which are found in fire extinguishers, aerosol sprays, and refrigerators, among other useful inventions, has sent additional, new forms of greenhouse gases into the atmosphere. CFCs reduce the amount of ozone in the atmosphere, and ozone protects Earth from the Sun's ultraviolet radiation.

Many fear that the reckless use of industry's beneficial inventions (after all, fire extinguishers put out destructive fires and fossil fuels run engines, factories, and power plants) will destroy the delicate balance of greenhouse gases. If too much heat is retained within Earth's atmosphere, the surface temperature will rise, causing massive environmental change, which can ultimately lead to extinction of many organisms.

What does deforestation have to do with the greenhouse effect?

Massive deforestation—the clearing of Earth's forests, including the rain forests—has limited Earth's natural ability to turn carbon dioxide into oxygen through photosynthesis. Forests are destroyed for a variety of reasons: fuel, land development, and precious woods, for example.

From 1980 to 1990, over 48 million acres of forest on 3 continents have been destroyed.

Deforestation also increases soil erosion, clogging streams and lakes with silt. Deforestation causes the land to heat and cool more quickly than before, which creates vast changes in Earth's interconnected weather system. Many animals are left without habitats or food sources when forests are cleared—especially in the rain forest where the number and variety of animal life exceeds that of any other place on Earth, except in the ocean.

How can Earth survive if it is so delicately balanced?

On one hand, Earth and its atmosphere are finely balanced ecologically. There is just enough oxygen; water is recycled; the weather distributes warm and cool air and water. It seems as though the planet is a delicately tuned instrument—even fragile.

On the other hand, Earth has existed for over 4 billion years. Floods, volcanoes, mass animal extinctions come and go, and have an importance in maintaining the planet. Asteroids have slammed into Earth. Disease has wiped out whole populations. But Earth still exists.

Our perspective is skewed by the relatively minute amount of time we humans live. Our innate nature causes us care for Earth: the life on it; the substances of it; and the processes and events that occur as a result of it. This is our incredible Earth.

What is air pressure?

Air is made up of molecules of different gases such as nitrogen and oxygen in constant, random motion. The molecules exert pressure whenever they hit a surface, but there aren't many surfaces in the air for them to hit, except each other. Air pressure is the result of colliding molecules. The frequency of molecular collisions determines the level of pressure: high pressure or low pressure. Rising pressure generally means fair weather. Falling air pressure signals the likelihood of storms.

What is warm air pressure like?

Warm air has fast-moving molecules. The force of their impact upon collision is great, but when they collide, the power of the impact sends them shooting far away, expanding the atmosphere as they go. As the atmosphere expands, it is less likely that these randomly moving molecules will hit each other. They have more room in which to roam uninterrupted. The frequency of impact is more important than the force of impact. Low pressure, there-

Fast-moving, high-impact, infrequently colliding molecules = warm, low air pressure.

fore, results from hot air: molecules moving quickly, but not colliding frequently in the expanding atmosphere.

What is cool air pressure like?

Slow-moving, low-impact, frequently colliding molecules = cool, high air pressure.

Molecules move more slowly in cool air than in warm air. They still travel randomly and they still collide with each other, but the impact of their collisions is not so great because they are moving slowly. Because the impact of collision is minimal, the molecules don't travel far (in fact, the atmosphere contracts in cold air), and have more of a chance of running into each other. The frequency of their collisions is much greater than that of warm-air molecules. Since air pressure is determined primarily by the frequency of contact, rather than the force of contact, cold air produces high air pressure.

How is air pressure measured?

The most common instrument used to measure air pressure is a barometer. A barometer is a vertical vacuum tube that sits with one open end in a pool of mercury. When the air exerts a high amount of pressure on the pool of mercury, the mercury rises up inside the tube. If the air pressure is low, the mercury does not rise so far inside the tube.

What is the relationship between air pressure and humidity?

Humidity is the amount of water vapor in the air. (Remember that water vapor is a gas, not a liquid.) Air has many different kinds of molecules: nitrogen, oxygen, and water vapor, for example. Nitrogen molecules are heavier than oxygen molecules and oxygen molecules are heavier than water vapor molecules. Nitrogen and oxygen molecules collide with other molecules forcefully, whereas the lighter water vapor's collisions are less powerful. The water vapor molecules don't travel far after a collision, so they collide more frequently. Therefore, as humidity increases (more water vapor in the air), air pressure decreases, and as humidity decreases, air pressure increases.

How do winds form?

Basically, wind is caused by two (or more) masses of air with different air pressure running into each other. High pressure areas always move toward adjoining low pressure areas. The attempt to equalize the pressure between the different air masses results in wind.

On a small scale, consider air over a shoreline. During the day, the ground releases more absorbed insolation (incoming solar radiation—sunshine) than does the water. Though they may receive the same amount of insolation, the water retains more of it. The air above the ground is heated by the released insolation and rises while its pressure sinks (hot air rises and hot air has low pressure). The air above the water remains cooler and has higher pressure. Since high-pressure areas try to infiltrate low-pressure masses, a cool wind, called a **sea breeze**, comes ashore from the water. At night, the water still has heat it absorbed during the day while the ground has already released a lot of its supply. The air over the water, then, becomes warmer with lower pressure than the air over land. Following the rule that high pressure seeks to replace low pressure, the wind shifts and a **land breeze** blows out to sea.

What are global winds?

Global winds also occur because large high- and low-pressure zones alternate from the North Pole to the South Pole about every 30° latitude (north-south location). Both poles have high-pressure air masses (cold, dry, high pressure) and the air above the equator is a low-pressure zone (hot, moist, low pressure). Because high pressure always invades low pressure, the resulting winds—where the high- and low-pressure zones meet—are pretty reliable. They are known as the **polar easterlies** (at 60° latitude north and south); the **westerlies** or prevailing winds (at 30° latitude north and south); and the **tropical easterlies** or trade winds (at the equator, 0° latitude).

What are fronts?

A front is the leading edge of a moving mass of uniformly cool or warm air. Under stable conditions, a mass, or area, of air will take on common characteristics of

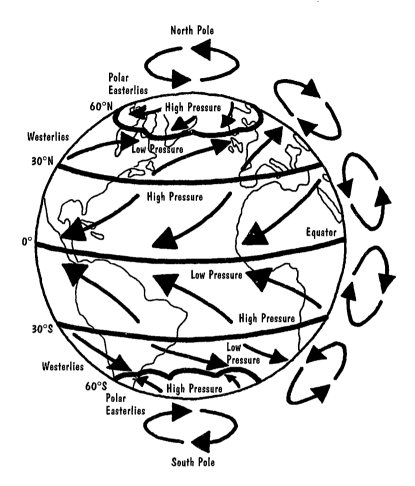

North Pole

Polar
Easterlies
60°N   High Pressure
Westerlies   Low Pressure
30°N
High Pressure
0°   Equator
Low Pressure
High Pressure
30°S
Low
Westerlies   Pressure
60°S   High Pressure
Polar
Easterlies

South Pole

Earth has certain predictable patterns of winds called prevailing winds. The air temperature at the equator is warmer than the air north and south of it. This difference in temperature is a major cause of Earth's global winds. The arrows showing circles above the surface of the Earth are convection cells, the atmospheric circulation of warm and cool air.

temperature, humidity, and pressure. The mass then moves as a unit according to the general circulation patterns around the world.

Different masses move at different speeds. Fronts are where two masses catch up or run into each other. Based on the properties of temperature, humidity, and pressure, the clashing fronts create relatively standard weather patterns.

What happens when a cold front moves in?

A cold front advancing on a warmer air mass will force the warm air mass upward (cold air sinks and hot air rises). The warm air rushes quickly upward causing rapid cooling and condensation of water vapor. In summer, thunderstorms will often accompany fast-rising warm air; in winter, a snowstorm can form. Once the cold front has pushed its way under the warm air, the surface temperature in that region will drop sharply.

What are the consequences of a warm front?

A warm front catching up to a cold front will ride up and over the tail end of the cold air. This causes condensation in the warm front since it is reaching higher and colder altitudes. The movement is relatively gradual, however, so widespread rain or snow results rather than abrupt storms.

What is a stationary front?

Sometimes two air masses meet up with each other, but neither is going anywhere. This is called a stationary front. Over time, the warm air at the front will rise up over the cold and the resulting weather is the same as a warm

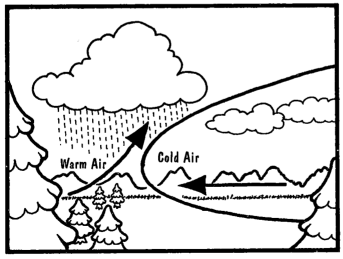

This cold front moving in on a warm front forces the warm air mass to rise. Precipitation often results when this happens, because the warm air mass cools as it rises and cannot hold the moisture it contains.

front: widespread precipitation. Rain or snow will persist, however, until another, more forceful, front comes to move the stationary front along.

What is an occluded front?

An occluded front consists of three fronts ganging up: a cool front followed by a warm front followed by a faster-moving cool front. What happens depends on the temperatures of the three fronts. Warm air will always rise, usually causing precipitation as its water vapor cools and condenses into clouds.

If the first air mass is cool and the third air mass is cold, the front is called a cold front occlusion. The colder, fast-moving front scoops up the warm air and then raises the tail end of the cool air mass. Along the front three layers form: from top to bottom, warm air, cool air, cold air.

In the reverse—a warm front occlusion—when the rear front is cool and the first mass is cold, the incoming cool air will rise up over the tail end of the cold air mass and wedge in between the cold and warm air. The layers still come out to warm, cool, and cold, top to bottom.

Occluded fronts cause both widespread and abrupt precipitation. Abrupt storms form as the warm air rapidly shoots upward, cools, and condenses. The more general precipitation occurs as the cool air is gradually lifted, cools further, and precipitates.

How is weather predicted?

There are now three basic methods of predicting weather. The first, **synoptic forecasting**, combines information from weather stations within a region and extrapolates, or takes from that information, likely weather patterns. The data is studied by meteorologists who use computers

Wind Chill

Wind chill has become a common winter statistic in weather forecasts. It is based on the fact that a windy cold day feels far colder to living creatures than a windless one. In fact, at frigid temperatures, wind can make the difference between life and death. A −40° Fahrenheit (−40° Celsius) calm day can be less hazardous than a 32° Fahrenheit (0° Celsius) day with a strong wind. To determine wind chill, all you need to do is multiply the wind speed by 1.5 and subtract it from the temperature.

Beaufort Scale of Wind

Beaufort Number	Wind	Speed (feet/meters per second)	(mph/kph)
0	Calm	< 1 / < 1	< ½ / < 1
1	Light air	1–5 / 30.5 cm–1.5 m	½–3½ / 1–5.6
2	Light breeze	5–11 / 1.5–3.3	3½–7½ / 5.6–12
3	Gentle breeze	11–17¾ / 3.3–5.4	7½–12 / 12–19.2
4	Moderate breeze	17¾–26 / 5.4–8	12–17¾ / 19.2–28.4
5	Fresh breeze	26–35 / 8–10.6	17¾–24 / 28.4–38.4
6	Strong breeze	35–45 / 10.6–13.7	24–30½ / 38.4–48.8
7	Near gale	45–56 / 13.7–17	30½–38 / 48.8–60.8
8	Gale	56–68 / 17–20.7	38–46 / 60.8–73.6
9	Strong gale	68–80 / 20.7–24.4	46–55 / 73.6–88
10	Storm	80–93 / 24.4–28.3	55–64 / 88–102.4
11	Violent storm	93–107 / 28.3–32.6	64–73 / 102.4–116.8
12	Hurricane	> 107 / > 32.6	> 73 / >116.8

to generate short-term predictions of wind, temperature, air pressure, and humidity changes, and possible storm fronts.

Statistical forecasting is based on historical knowledge of weather and its patterns in a given area. Meteorologists apply mathematical equations created from studying past weather patterns to foretell likely changes in the next 5 to 90 days.

Numerical forecasting stems from the knowledge of physics and the atmosphere. Mathematical equations are drawn from the physical laws of nature, such as Newton's laws of motion and thermodynamics (the conservation of energy), applied to weather conditions. Computers work out the mathematics—the equations were impossible to solve in a timely fashion before computers existed—and the information is primarily used for 5-day forecasts.

Why are weather predictions so often wrong?

Computers, satellites, and scientists are no match for the variables that exist in nature. Human error, statistical error, and mechanical error all have a part in weather forecasts going wrong, but even if all the people, information, and instruments were perfect, it would still be impossible to be 100 percent correct.

Our understanding of the intricate relationships between the atmosphere and land and water is far from complete. Weather forecasting is an attempt—and a much more successful one now than 50 years ago—to lay out what we do know and discuss the probable progression of the current situation. Thousands of lives have been saved by forecasting hurricanes, floods, storms, and extreme temperatures. But weather, if nothing else, will keep us humble in the face of nature.

What is a weather station?

Thousands of weather stations are set up around the world. Meteorologists there gather information from satellites, computers, each other, and individuals in remote areas. By coordinating their information, they can track and predict the weather worldwide.

How do all those weather stations communicate?

In this age of global communication—with telephone, telegraph, satellites, and computers—it is not difficult for meteorologists to exchange information. A relatively primitive, but useful, tool they use is a station model. These symbols give a summary of weather in shorthand. Once you know how to interpret it, you can share their information, too.

What are the lines and squiggles on weather maps?

Once you know what these mean, reading weather maps is relatively simple. The lines, called **isobars**, which form concentric circles, outline the pressure zones. An H or an L will frequently be seen in the middle of the zones, designating a high- or low-pressure area. The numbers along the lines give you the barometric readings.

The squiggles, or **isotherms**, are simply lines connecting the same temperature over a wide area. For instance, if it is 50° Fahrenheit (10° Celsius) in Seattle, Washington; Butte, Montana; Chicago, Illinois; Cincinnati,

Ohio; and Charleston, South Carolina, a wavy line marked 50° will be drawn connecting those cities. A number of these lines on a map will outline the temperatures and give you an idea of what may be coming, given the winds, storm systems, and pressure zones.

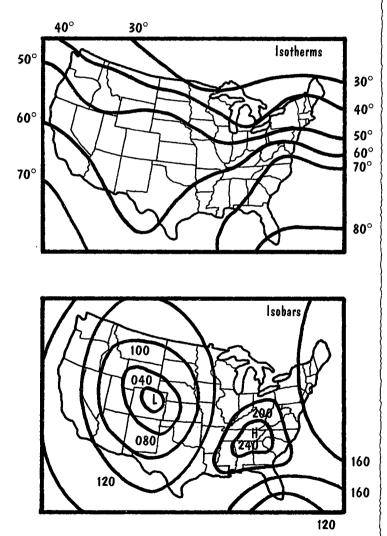

Isotherms show areas with the same air temperature. Isobars show areas with the same air pressure.

How do clouds form?

Condensation, gas changing to liquid, is the foundation of cloud formation. When warm, generally moist air rises, it cools. When there are particles in the air for the water vapor to adhere to, the vapor converts to water droplets, between 0.02 and 0.6 millimeters (0.000788 and 0.02364 inches) wide. The particles, which can be dust, pollutants, ice or salt crystals, or chemical compounds, are called **condensation nuclei**. Without them, the water vapor either remains gaseous or converts directly to ice crystals through **sublimation**. Sublimation is the process of a gas turning into a solid without going through the liquid stage. Given cold enough temperatures, water vapor will instantly crystallize. The resultant ice crystals provide condensation nuclei for the vapor to condense on.

How cold are clouds?

Clouds below −100° Fahrenheit (−73° Celsius) are completely ice.

Water droplets remain liquid in clouds down to −27° Fahrenheit (−32° Celsius), far below freezing. They remain in a liquid state because of the high pressure in the atmosphere. The temperature must fall below −80° Fahrenheit (−70° Celsius) before the droplets crystallize into ice.

What is fog?

Fog occurs when rising water vapor turns to droplets at ground level. Essentially, fog is simply a very low-lying cloud. Fog, or mist, often appears early in the morning, but as the surface temperature rises, it evaporates.

What is dew?

Condensation of water vapor on the ground produces dew. Grass, flowers, trees, stones, and anything else on the ground provides plenty of condensation nuclei, or surfaces for water vapor to condense on. Frost is simply colder, frozen dew.

What is dew point?

Dew point is the temperature at which water vapor liquefies. It signifies that the air is filled to capacity with moisture. Like a cloud, the water vapor becomes too heavy to stay suspended in air. It needs a surface on which to condense. Since the vapor is hovering at ground level, there is a great supply of surfaces, or condensation nuclei, including grass, stones, plants, and animals.

How is humidity measured?

There are two instruments which measure dew point. The first is a hygrometer. This tool is made of human hair. Hair lengthens and shrinks with humidity, growing longer in moist air. A pointer attached to the hair changes position along a scale as the hair gets longer and shorter.

The second instrument is a psychrometer. Two thermometers are used, one kept out in the air and one whose bulb is immersed in water. The dry thermometer measures the air temperature. The wet thermometer measures the air temperature cooled by the rate of evaporation, or the ability of the air to take up more water. The relationship between the air temperature and the difference between the temperatures of the two thermometers is plotted on a relative humidity chart, giving the percentage of moisture in the air.

How many different kinds of clouds exist?

There are probably infinite shapes which clouds can form, given all the variables in the atmosphere, but three basic shapes are used to classify clouds. **Cumulus** clouds are the flat-bottomed, tall clouds that look like whipped cream or cauliflower. Thick layers of clouds, like blankets in the sky, are called **stratus** clouds. **Cirrus** clouds tend to be high in the air, small, thin, and wispy.

Clouds can exhibit characteristics of more than one type, and more than one kind of cloud can be in the sky at any time. When clouds have combined traits, their names are generally made up by joining the names of the different clouds. For instance, cirrostratus clouds have the height of cirrus clouds and something of the shape of stratus clouds.

Clouds likely to precipitate are called **nimbus**, as in **cumulonimbus** (cumulus rain-snow clouds) or **strato-nimbus** (stratus rain-snow clouds). Cirrus clouds are frequently too thin to accumulate enough condensation to cause precipitation.

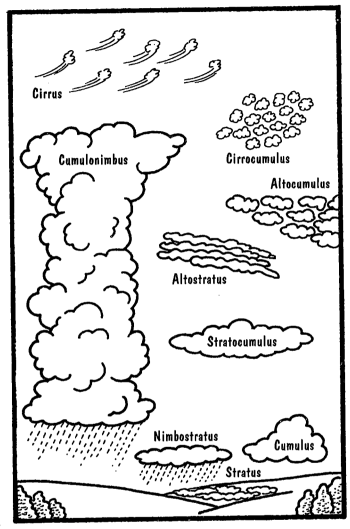

The three main types of clouds are cirrus, cumulus, and stratus.
Clouds can be combinations or variations on these three types.
Nimbus or Nimbo signals likely precipitation. Alto means high.

How far up in the air do clouds form?

Most clouds stay in the troposphere, the 10-mile (16-kilometer) layer of the atmosphere nearest Earth. Clouds are classified by height as well as shape. Cumulus clouds of fair weather, congested cumulus, and the lower parts of a cumulonimbus cloud will all form below about 6,500 feet (1,981 meters), along with stratus, stratonimbus, and stratocumulus.

The family of midheight clouds include altocumulus (high cumulus), altostratus (high stratus), and the midsection of cumulonimbus. The middle section extends up to 23,000 feet (7,010 meters) above Earth's surface.

High clouds, above 23,000 feet (7,010 meters), are cirrus, cirrocumulus, cirrostratus, and the top of cumulonimbus. Yes, the cumulonimbus can reach through all three layers of the troposphere. They can actually poke their way into the stratosphere, growing as tall as 65,000 feet (19,812 meters).

What are fair-weather cumulus clouds like?

Cumulus clouds of fair weather generally occur in late morning or early afternoon on a fair day. "Bubbles" of air warmed by Earth's surface rise and condense in discreet clouds about 1,500 to 4,000 feet (457 to 1,219 meters) in the air. The clouds are separated by sinking cooler air, but the weather is generally stable or settled if there are fair-weather cumulus in the sky.

How do stratus clouds form?

Stratus appear when warm air is rising in layers instead of bubbles. This produces wide cloud bases because a stretch of air is reaching the condensation point at the same time. They are generally rather thin, under 10,000 feet (3,048 meters) in the air. Fog is a stratus cloud that hovers at surface level. Rolling fog comes from a mass of warmer air moving horizontally along a cooler surface, such as a pond or lake, or land that has been cooled overnight.

What is the difference between stratus and altostratus clouds?

Altostratus clouds occur higher in the atmosphere, between 10,000 and 20,000 feet (3,048 and 6,096 meters) up. They frequently form on top of a warm front moving in on top of a cooler mass of air. The cool air mass acts the same as land in the production of stratus clouds.

From a person's vantage point on Earth, altostratus clouds can cover the whole sky. They are generally only 1,300 to 5,000 feet (396 to 1,524 meters) thick, but can range over a 600-mile (960-kilometer) wide area. If the water droplets in altostratus are on the large side, they can produce a cloud cover that either obscures sunlight or blocks the Sun from view entirely.

What makes cirrostratus different from other stratus clouds?

Cirrostratus clouds form high in the sky, about 20,000 feet (6,096 meters) or higher. They are made up of ice crystals rather than liquid droplets. While from Earth cirrostratus appear so thin as to be almost invisible, airplane pilots have documented thicknesses around 10,000 feet (3,048 meters)—like a thick ice fog in the sky.

How can a cloud be cumulus and stratus at the same time?

A stratocumulus cloud is evidence of two simultaneous types of air circulation: warm air rising, cooling, and sinking in small independent cells high in the sky and more stable warm air rising from Earth's surface. The more stable, wider mass of warm air rising from the surface creates a layer of stratus clouds. Above that, the more frantic circulation of convection cells builds cumulus towers of condensation on top of it.

What are altocumulus clouds?

A sky full of cirrocumulus is sometimes called a mackerel sky, after the small fish.

Sometimes the sky looks like it is filled with popcorn. The pieces of popcorn are actually independent heaping cumulus clouds that form on top of a stable air mass between 10,000 and 20,000 feet (3,048 and 6,096 meters) in the air. Above this layer the atmosphere must be full of moisture and small circular movements of warmer and cooler air rising and sinking to create the mounting puffs of cumulus clouds. The spaces in between the popcorn pieces are evidence of cool, dry air sinking. The clouds themselves show that the warmer air is rising, cooling, and condensing.

What are cirrocumulus clouds?

Basically, cirrocumulus are altocumulus, only higher in the atmosphere, above 28,000 feet (8,534 meters). They are also formed by cells of warm and cooling air and pockets of sinking cool air that let the blue sky show through, but the cells are smaller—and higher—than those that create altocumulus. Cirrocumulus look different from altocumulus, more like carpet or fish scales than popcorn.

What is an anvil cumulonimbus?

First, a cumulonimbus is a cumulus cloud that produces precipitation, rain, snow, hail, or sleet. Anvil refers to the shape of a blacksmith's anvil, which is a wide surface on top of a thinner base. A blacksmith pounds hot metals on the top surface of an anvil. The anvil shape forms on top of a cumulonimbus (or a cumulus) because a wide stable mass of cold air in the atmosphere prevents the cloud from growing further in its usual fashion. Usually, the small cells of warmer air rising and condensing within the cloud form billows that heap on top of each other, but the cold mass on top acts as a ceiling. The condensation spreads outward below the ceiling instead of upward.

Are all clouds some form of cumulus, stratus, or cirrus?

Given the many variables of our atmosphere, you might imagine that not all clouds could fit in standard categories. You would be right. There are probably infinite shapes, densities, temperatures, and colors of clouds. Many varieties may occur without anyone ever even noticing them! Some unusual clouds, including banners, caps, and lenticular altocumulus, result from air passing over peculiar land forms.

Banners, caps, and lenticular altocumulus all form as a result of mountains affecting air currents. The names banners and caps describe two shapes of clouds that are caused by dry, high-pressure air hitting humid, low-pressure air sitting on top of a mountain peak.

Lenticular altocumulus means a high cumulus cloud in the shape of a lens, or two contact lenses cupped together and filled with cloud. These bizarre clouds form at the crest of a breaking wave of air over a mountain

Lenticular altocumulus clouds look remarkably like UFOs we've seen in the movies.

peak or ridge. From there, they can sail off into the sky, keeping their otherworldly shape.

What are noctilucent clouds?

Noctilucent clouds appear at twilight or dawn and appear to be brilliantly colored in neon light. These clouds are not reflecting city lights. Water droplets condense on meteoric particles about 50 miles (80 kilometers) above Earth. The light of the setting or rising Sun passes through the water to the metallic components of the particles, making the clouds glow in luminescent colors of the rainbow.

What is the difference between rain and drizzle?

Drizzle differs from rain in rate of precipitation and size of droplets. Both forms of precipitation occur as water droplets in clouds join until they are too heavy to remain airborne. Drizzle is very fine droplets. The fine droplets fall very close together and very slowly, compared to rain.

Is snow just frozen rain?

It may be easy to explain snow as frozen rain, but it isn't really true. Snow has never been rain. Water vapor in extremely cold temperatures sublimes, or passes directly from a gas to a solid, into ice crystals, which consequently form clouds. Snow precipitates out of clouds in the same way rain does: When the mass of crystals becomes dense enough, gravity pulls it toward Earth.

What is sleet?

Sleet, not snow, is accurately described as frozen rain. Water vapor condenses into water droplets, forming clouds and precipitating. The rain droplets crystallize as they fall through atmosphere that is below freezing. By the time sleet reaches the ground, the droplets are pellets of ice.

What is glaze?

Supercooled rain—rain that remains liquid even in freezing temperatures because of massive pressure—hitting a surface that is below freezing creates a coating a sheer ice. That is glaze.

What are ice storms?

We commonly refer to storms of glaze as ice storms, when every inch (centimeter) of every surface is covered in ice. The ice conforms to the shape of the surface—not only rooftops, streets, and library steps, but even the surfaces of twigs, telephone wires, and car antennas. The whole environment seems made of ice; it is an amazing sight.

How is hail produced?

Hail, one of the most destructive forms of precipitation, goes through a relatively lengthy evolution. It can begin as either rain or snow, but then proceeds through layers of atmosphere that alternate between above and below freezing. Because of the changing temperature, there are forceful updrafts of wind that reverse the course of the hail back upward. The hail freezes, partially thaws, refreezes, and partially thaws, on and on as it travels back and forth through the layers of atmosphere. With each trip, the hailstone grows in size until it finally makes its way through the entire atmosphere to Earth's surface.

How large can a hailstone grow?

Hailstones can be as small as grains of rice or as big as softballs. The largest recorded hailstone measured 5.57 inches (14 centimeters) in diameter and weighed 1.67 pounds (759 grams).

How destructive are hail storms?

Regardless of its size, hail can be a devastatingly destructive force, wiping out whole crops and shattering windows. If you've ever been caught out in a good hailstorm, you know for yourself the painful stinging of being relentlessly pelted by ice.

According to a Kansas newspaper, the largest hailstone in recorded history fell like a "shot from the sky" in Coffeyville, on September 3, 1970.

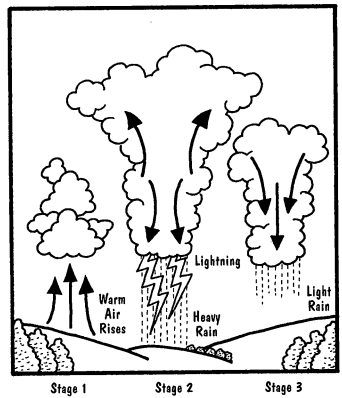

Stage 1   Stage 2   Stage 3

Thunderstorms occur in warm weather when moist air rises very quickly and cools.

What are thunderstorms?

Thunderstorms are relatively common weather phenomena. In one sense, you probably know what they are:
loud, wet storms, sometimes furious, sometimes with
bright flashes of lightning. Thunderstorms grow when a
convection cell (circulating warm and cooling, condensing air) in the atmosphere rises quickly as a result of
intense heat. The air can rise miles high in a matter of
minutes, which causes a great updraft. A rain cloud develops rapidly with the cooling air condensing into water
droplets or ice crystals until they become heavy enough
for gravity to pull them back toward Earth.

What is thunder?

Thunder is not the sound of lightning or the sound of clouds bumping into each other. The heat of lightning literally explodes the air around it. Thunder is the sound of the explosion. We actually can't hear a large part of the thunder because the sound waves fall below our hearing threshold.

How does thunder roll?

The sound of rolling thunder, an extended noise that seems to move, is a result of the fact that sound travels relatively slowly. Thunder comes from air exploding in the intense heat of lightning. A lightning bolt may travel as far as 2 miles (3 kilometers) at a rate of about 93,000 miles (148,800 kilometers) per second. At ground level, sound travels about a mile (1.6 kilometers) in 5 seconds.

It has been said that it would take 200 million trumpeters blasting for 13 seconds to reproduce the amount of noise in one peal of thunder.

Thunderstorm Mythology

Changes in weather have frequently been credited to religious figures: gods, goddesses, and holy men and women. Many ancient civilizations connected thunder and lightning with their gods. The reigning monarchs of Roman, Greek, and Norse mythology—Jupiter, Zeus, and Thor, respectively—all held lightning bolts as symbols of their power. All three were known for flinging them about in anger, too. Thunder came from Thor's hammer. Popular Christian mythology held angels responsible for rain, raindrops being angels' tears. Also some claim that on Good Friday, the holiday commemorating Jesus Christ's death, between the hours of 1 and 3 o'clock, the sky darkens and rain frequently falls. The Old Testament relates many stories of weather-related miracles. Moses parts the Red Sea; manna, or holy bread, falls from heaven; fires burst out for no apparent reason other than to show Yahweh's power; and in retaliation for their wickedness, Yahweh drowns all living creatures—except those aboard Noah's Ark—in a great flood.

Weather, in fact, does have immense power to bring good and bad to people. People have not been able to tame it. Even today, with all of our understanding and technology, weather still brings mass destruction as well as the sunshine and water for life and growth—regardless of what we want it to do.

So what we hear as a roll of thunder is simply the delayed noise of the lightning traveling. It sounds as if it is traveling because it is.

Why do we see lightning before hearing thunder?

Light and sound travel at different speeds. Light waves travel about 186,000 miles (297,600 kilometers) per second. The distance they must travel to reach our eyes from a cloud is covered in a tiny fraction of a second. We say we see lightning instantly because our senses cannot distinguish the infinitesimal amount of time it actually takes for the light to reach our eyes.

The sound waves of thunder, on the other hand, travel about 1 mile (1.6 kilometers) every 5 seconds at ground level. Therefore, we register the sight of lightning long before we register the sound of the exploding air caused by lightning.

How can you gauge the distance of a thunderstorm?

It is true that you can gauge the distance of a storm by counting the seconds between the time you see a flash of lightning and hear thunder. Every five seconds between the two events means the lightning bolt is 1 mile (1.6 kilometers) away. If you see lightning and 20 seconds later you hear thunder, the lightning was 4 miles (6.4 kilometers) away.

What is lightning?

In a storm, the rapidly rising air causes updrafts. Downdrafts result when gravity takes over, causing the condensed air to fall in water droplets, snow, or hail. The friction between the updrafts and downdrafts creates static electricity that discharges as lightning.

How big is a bolt of lightning?

Lightning tends to be long and skinny. The central ray of electricity in a lightning bolt can travel more than 2 miles (3 kilometers), whether down toward Earth, horizontally, or upward into the higher atmosphere. The bolt is usually only 6 inches (15 centimeters) in diameter, and often much less. The surrounding brightness of the flash extends further, but technically it is not part of the lightning. It comes from the heating of air particles around the lightning bolt.

Why does lightning strike?

The friction of drafts in clouds produces a negative charge at the bottom of a cloud and a positive charge at the top. Because opposite charges attract each other, the negative charges attract the positive charges on the ground. When the charging electrical force between the cloud and ground reaches 3 million volts, the air becomes a conductor (a substance through which electricity travels). The electrical current shoots down from the cloud, strikes Earth, and Earth sends the electrical charge back up to the cloud. Offshoots of a lightning bolt form wherever the air is sufficiently charged to conduct the electricity.

Lightning is often accompanied by a ripping sound. Imagine the static electricity when you pull off a sweater. It crackles. That is the same sound of electricity that lightning makes, only in much greater magnitude.

A sulfurous smell is associated with lightning. The smell results from chemical reactions in the air, creating ozone and nitrous oxides.

What happens when lightning strikes?

The consequences of lightning striking depends on what it strikes. Certain materials conduct, or channel, electricity better than others. Water, for instance is a good electrical conductor, which is why you should never swim outside during an electrical storm. People—and other living things—conduct electricity, but enough electricity will kill them. Lightning will frequently set fire to trees, houses, fields, and other combustible materials.

What are the different kinds of lightning?

Lightning generally comes in bolts and sheets. Lightning bolts are lines of electricity passing through the atmosphere. Sheet lightning appears as flashes of light in

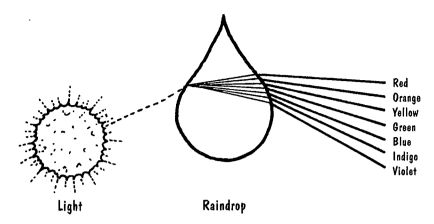

Red
Orange
Yellow
Green
Blue
Indigo
Violet

Light   Raindrop

When sunlight hits water droplets at a certain angle, we see a rainbow. The droplets separate the sunlight into the different colors of the visible spectrum, just like a prism does.

the sky. There really is no difference in the lightning itself, simply in how we see it. When lightning occurs shielded from our sight by cloud cover, we see its reflection as a momentary flash of light.

What causes a rainbow?

Rainbows occur as a result of sunlight being refracted and reflected by raindrops (or mist or spray). To see a rainbow, you must have your back to the Sun and there must be sunlight as well as rain. The sunlight that strikes drops of rain is literally bent as it enters the liquid. When sunlight bends, as when it shines through a prism, the light separates into the spectrum of colors: red, orange, yellow, green, blue, indigo, and violet. The light bounces off the back walls of the raindrops and is bent again, mirroring the spherical shape of the water droplet in an arc, or bow.

The sunlight, the rain, and the observer's line of sight must form an approximate 42° angle for a rainbow to be visible. It is at this angle that the reflected, refracted light can be seen. A double rainbow is the result of the water droplets being large enough that the sunlight reflects twice within the raindrop before becoming a rainbow. An angle of about 52° is needed for a double rainbow.

What are the differences between hurricanes, cyclones, and typhoons?

These three words all describe the same phenomenon: a tropical storm of fierce spiraling winds. Such storms occur around the world, but only between the equator and latitudes 30° north and south of it. When these storms occur in the Atlantic Ocean, they are called hurricanes. They are called cyclones in the Indian Ocean and typhoons in the Pacific Ocean. Cyclone is also a generic word for a whirlpool of wind.

In Australia, tropical storms of fierce spiraling winds are also known as willy-willies.

What causes a hurricane?

Hurricanes result from an increasingly strong storm system over water. When air over warm ocean water is heated by the Sun to about 81° Fahrenheit (27° Celsius), it rises in severely increased updrafts and low pressure. Numerous, large convection cells (circulation patterns of warm air rising, cooling, and condensing) go to work creating a widespread storm, lowering the air pressure more and more. The cells merge and great winds begin to blow as surrounding high pressure air moves in to equalize the low pressure. Winds tend to blow in the same direction, clockwise in the Northern Hemisphere and counterclockwise in the Southern Hemisphere, which creates a whirlpool, or cyclone. Meanwhile, the

Hurricanes can grow to be over 1,000 miles (1,600 kilometers) wide with wind speeds of 200 miles (320 kilometers) per hour.

Hurricane Names

In Chinese, *ta-feng* means "violent winds." A mispronunciation of this word became the name for the violent cyclones in the Pacific Ocean: typhoons. The generic term *cyclone* was coined in 1844 and was meant to call to mind the whirling image of a coiled, striking snake. The word *hurricane* comes from the language of an extinct West Indian tribe, the Taino. *Huracan* meant "evil spirit" and was associated with the God of Evil who sent wind storms to punish people.

The custom of naming hurricanes began at least 150 years ago. Early names were taken from Christian saints traditionally honored the day a hurricane happened to take place. The 1825 hurricane Santa Ana was named for Saint Ann. From 1953 to 1979, hurricanes were christened with female names, beginning with the letter A and proceeding through the alphabet. One impact of the feminist revolution in the 1970s was to begin using male as well as female names. Now the names run through the alphabet alternating male and female.

convection cell is constantly fed by the heat of condensing air and the wind, growing larger and stronger. When the winds reach a speed of about 75 miles (120 kilometers) per hour, the storm has become a hurricane.

Are hurricanes only wind storms?

Not only are hurricane winds ferocious, but vast amounts of rain pour down from the saturated clouds. In a single day, a hurricane can unleash as much precipitation as falls over a whole year in rainy Seattle, Washington.

The strong air currents of a hurricane also churn up vast amounts of ocean water, called **storm surges**, creating large waves weighing hundreds of tons. Coastal damage from these giant waves can easily equal or surpass the devastation of a hurricane's winds.

What is the eye of a hurricane?

A hurricane is a spiral of winds racing up to 200 miles (320 kilometers) per hour, but in the middle of the whirlpool lies a calm center called the eye. As unbelievable as it sounds, the sheer force of the storm in its spiral formation allows some 10 to 30 miles (16 to 48 kilometers) at the center to remain unaffected. The weather within the eye of a hurricane is warm, still, and cloudless.

What causes a tornado?

A tornado evolves similarly to a hurricane. When the earth's surface is warm enough, the air rises with great speed, causing intense low pressure and increased temperatures. (The weather conditions are usually right in summer, though tornadoes have been recorded throughout the year.) Cooler surrounding air with higher pressure rushes in, creating strong **convection cells** (circulation patterns of warm air rising, cooling, condensing, and sinking). Because strong winds form a spiral, the rushing updrafts begin to spin, forming a funnel.

The funnel of a tornado forms in the sky and grows downward. As it nears the ground, it picks up dust and debris, which allow us to see the swirling winds. The moving air further decreases the pressure within the tornado, feeding the updrafts and accelerating the wind speed.

How big are tornadoes?

The funnel clouds formed by tornadoes can reach up to 2,000 feet (610 meters) across at the narrow end. Since they form from cloud bases, theoretically they can be up to 6,500 feet (1,981 meters) tall, though we don't really have any way of measuring them. The winds inside funnels reach as high as 370 miles (592 kilometers) per hour.

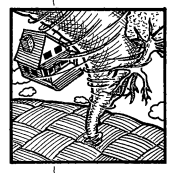

What damage do tornadoes cause?

Tornadoes do not always reach Earth's surface, but given enough strength, the point of the funnel touches down. The winds devour almost anything in their path by sucking them up into the funnel, whirling them around, and sending them crashing back to Earth. Stories abound of objects such as train cars being lifted, rotated, and returned to Earth; forks and bicycles being embedded in trees; whole lakes—fish, plants, and all—being sucked into the funnel.

A 1917 tornado in Texas spun out of control for 7 hours.

Tornado damage results not only from severe winds and blowing debris, but from drastic low pressure. Objects, such as houses, caught in a tornado's path can literally explode because the air pressure within them is so

Most tornadoes happen in the United States and most of them occur in a path from northern Texas, up through Oklahoma, Kansas, and Nebraska. The frequency of tornadoes here has earned this swath of land the nickname Tornado Alley.

much higher than the tornado's. Air pressure constantly tries to even itself out. The seemingly odd safety precaution of opening windows when a tornado approaches makes good sense. It helps to even out the pressure.

Do tornadoes have eyes?

The eye of a tornado, like the eye of a hurricane, is merely the center of the funnel.

In 1928, a Kansas man by the name of Will Keller flattened himself to the ground as a tornado skipped over him. He watched the tornado as it passed over him, and what he saw added invaluable information to our knowledge of the insides of tornadoes.

In the few seconds it took for the tornado to pass, the air became strangely calm. Keller had difficulty breathing and heard a noise he described as a screaming, hissing sound coming from the funnel. The funnel opening above him was about 55 feet (17 meters) across and extended some 2,500 feet (762 meters) up. Toward the bottom of the tornado, Keller saw a number of small tornadoes form and dissipate. It would have been impossible to see anything because of the darkness except for constant bright flashes of lightning ricocheting off the interior walls of rotating wind and debris.

We see the swirling winds of a tornado because the wind picks up dust and debris. When a tornado occurs over water, it picks up water and forms a waterspout. Tornadoes produce the strongest winds found on Earth.

While pilots can fly airplanes through the eye of a hurricane—and they do, to study the phenomenon—tornadoes are too small, too spontaneous, and exist for too brief a time for close observation of the eye.

What is a waterspout?

When a tornado passes over a body of water, it may pull the entire contents of the pond into its funnel, creating a waterspout. The water as well as the animal and plant life enter the swirling winds and are scattered. Waterspouts are rare and rather awesome.

What is a mirage?

Mirages are tricks played on the eye by light. The most typical weather-related mirage is that of a shining pool of water in a hot desert. Bent sunlight creates this optical illusion on very hot ground. Surfaces that are heated to 120° Fahrenheit (49° Celsius), such as midday desert landscapes, radiate a thin (less dense) layer of very hot air that hovers over the ground. Above that layer rests a colder (more dense) air mass. As sunlight passes through the cold air to the hot, the rays are bent so that they reflect an image of the sky. The shimmering heat makes the reflection look like a pool of water.

Air masses can also cause cold-weather mirages. Frigid surfaces create a very cold layer of air just above the ground with a warmer layer above it. When the sunlight passes through the warmer layer to the cold, it bends, reflecting not the sky, but the surface just over the horizon. This fascinating trick can create whole towns that seem to float in the air.

What causes floods?

Floods result from many different situations. Flooding can follow volcanic activity and earthquakes. As Earth shifts, tsunamis race across oceans, and water vapor is released into the atmosphere. Hurricanes whip up merciless waves that cause flooding. Melting glaciers can raise the level of lakes and rivers beyond their boundaries, as can heavy, incessant rain or snow. Natural disasters, such as landslides, avalanches, natural dike breaks, and soil

The Johnstown Flood

The worst flood in United States history happened in Johnstown, Pennsylvania, on May 31, 1889. The town is situated on the South Fork of the Little Conemaugh River. The South Fork Dam, some 15 miles (24 kilometers) north of Johnstown, had been built in 1853, but fell into disrepair. The lake created by the dam was stocked with fish so that vacationers along its banks could enjoy fishing on their holidays. Wire screens were installed in front of the lake's outlets to prevent the fish from escaping. The screens became completely clogged with silt and aquatic plant growth, so that when heavy rains fell the night of May 30, 1889, the water had no natural release. The pressure of the mounting water broke the dam at 3 o'clock on May 31. A wall of water reaching 20 to 30 feet (6 to 9 meters) in the air rushed at a speed of 22 feet (7 meters) per second toward Johnstown. Within a matter of minutes, the town was flooded and most of its inhabitants were either dead or left homeless.

erosion, can bring on massive flooding. Of course, in civilization's attempt to make Earth conform to people's needs, we have created our own flood dangers. The famous flood in Johnstown, Pennsylvania, in 1889 seems to have been caused by vacation homeowners neglecting to repair the dikes along the lake created for their enjoyment.

What is a flash flood?

Flash floods can occur wherever land is unable to absorb rainfall or any torrent of water (such as a dam break) quickly enough to prevent water rising. They happen, as their name suggests, in a flash.

In urban areas, the presence of a lot of nonporous or less porous material—asphalt, cement, tar, and stone, for instance—inhibits large amounts of water from seeping into the ground. Low-lying areas, such as bridge underpasses, are especially susceptible to instant flooding as water from the environment gathers there.

In less populated areas, flash floods are as terrifying, because there are no sewer systems or other intentionally designed outlets for water runoff. Gorges, canyons, deserts, and ravines with relatively little porous material can be hit with flash floods during a violent storm, or even hours later and miles away from the torrent.

Water from a storm has to go somewhere. Even if the storm occurs 20 miles (32 kilometers) away and there is nowhere for the water to run, it will build up like a river, racing over the terrain until it reaches absorbent land or some water outlet. Water seeks lower levels, and deep ravines or gorges provide ideal channels for rushing water.

Are floods always disastrous?

Floods are generally natural occurrences, which means they are likely to have benefits for Earth, even if they are destructive to property or lives. Before a man-made dam system was built in Egypt, the Nile River flooded every year at the end of June. The event brought joy to the Egyptians after months of arid summer had dried up the land. The floods brought much needed irrigation and fertile silt for crops, as well as drinking, bathing, and swimming water. Floods in other dry climates—in China and Cambodia—have been seen as lifelines.

What are the best means of flood control?

People have developed many methods of controlling floods and using the water to their benefit. Reservoirs are built to hold excessive rain, and the water is used for agriculture and personal use. Channels to redirect floodwaters only work if they guide the water to its natural destination. Otherwise, they force the water to run deeper and more quickly, causing more erosion and damage. Government regulations have attempted to control floods, legislating the use of flood-plains, demanding reservoir, dam, and dike construction and repair, and keeping residents informed of rising waters.

Although not perfect, dikes and dams have proven to be the simplest and most effective devices of flood control. Walls of soil, rock, metals, brick, or even sandbags hold back floodwaters from populated areas. The

The Worst Flood in History

In September and October 1887, the 2,800-mile (4,480-kilometer)-long Hwang Ho River in China overflowed. Water rushed out over 70-foot (21-meter)-high barriers to flood about 50,000 square miles (129,534 square kilometers) of land. Estimates of fatalities range from 900,000 to 6 million. Over 2 million people were left homeless.

Netherlands has created an extensive dike system, critical to managing the flow of water through a country that is at or below sea level.

What is a drought?

A drought is a weather-related severe dry spell during which expected rain doesn't fall and groundwater seeps further down and away from the surface. Strong, dry winds, clear skies, and high temperatures tend to accompany droughts.

What causes a drought?

Scientists have noted that droughts frequently occur when the Sun displays numerous sunspots on its surface. No one is sure why.

Droughts may result from shifting wind patterns. An area that normally receives moist, steady breezes from the ocean will suffer if the variables of weather cause the winds to shift. Since land warms and dries faster than ocean, the lack of these winds can be devastating when combined with limited rainfall. If a high-pressure zone (warm and dry) persists over a region without anything to move it on, the likelihood of rain diminishes.

What are the effects of drought?

Limited water supply is devastating since life has always depended on its presence. People, animals, and plants all need water to survive.

Some animals, especially those who inhabit arid climates, have evolved physiological defenses against lack of water. The camel is probably the best-known drought-resistant animal. Contrary to popular opinion, camels do not carry water in their humps. The humps are a special kind of fat which supplies the camel with hydrogen. When this hydrogen mixes with the oxygen the camel breathes it forms water.

Plants have defense mechanisms that protect them against periodic dry spells. You have probably seen houseplants droop from lack of water. This is a sign that the plant's defenses are working. The pores of the plant are sealed to prevent evaporation. The plant goes into a sort of hibernation, slowing down its systems to expend less energy.

How long do droughts last?

While scientists have been able to establish some routine for the onset of droughts, their duration is less well understood. Droughts can last from a month to years. In some cases, droughts herald a complete climate change, turning a relatively temperate region into a desert.

What was the Dust Bowl?

From 1930 to 1937, the United States suffered its worst drought in history. Across 50 million acres (20.25 million hectares) of land in Kansas, Oklahoma, Texas, New Mexico, Colorado, Nebraska, and the Dakotas, dry weather and winds caused massive dust storms that carried particles as far as New York City. In 1933 and 1934, the storms were so bad that trains were stopped by dunes. Animals suffocated. Dust piled up on all surfaces and couldn't be kept out of homes. The air was so dense that the sky seemed black. Crops were covered with dust and failed to grow. The drought's persistence even caused the Great Lakes to set record-breaking low-water levels.

Can weather cause fires?

There are many different ways in which weather-related phenomenon cause fires. Burning lava from volcanoes sets towns aflame. Fires can be the most destructive part of earthquakes, though they only happen when earthquakes occur in populated areas. Earthquakes rupture gas lines and electrical wires, as was the case in the great San Francisco earthquake of 1906. Three-quarters of the city burned down.

Lightning bolts striking the planet can easily spark a fire, especially during a dry spell or a drought.

The wind not only fans fire, but can sometimes cause it. Two tree branches violently rubbing against each other during a drought can create enough friction to make sparks and the sparks can develop into flames.

Over 50 percent of the massive fires that occur in the western United States are caused by lightning.

GLOSSARY

A

abyssal plain the wide section of ocean floor that extends from the continental rise to the ocean ridge

acid rain rain that contains atmospheric impurities or pollution, such as nitric acid or sulfuric acid

annula the bright ring of the outer edge of the Sun's surface, sometimes visible during a solar eclipse

anticline deformation a bridge-shaped rock formation caused by underground stress

aquifer a layer of permeable rock from which water can be extracted

atmosphere the layer of gases surrounding a planet or satellite

axis an imaginary line through a celestial body around which the body rotates, or spins

B

basalt dark, dense rock of cooled lava

basement rock a mass of joined greenstone belts

bipedal walking upright on two legs

C

calcareous oozes decayed calcium animal shells on the ocean floor

capacity the amount of silt which a specific river is able to carry

carnivore; carnivorous a meat-eating animal; meat eating

cave a cavern or large space created within rock by erosion

celestial bodies objects in the solar system, such as planets, stars, satellites, and moons

cilia hairlike strands attached to the outer membrane wall of a cell whose rhythmic movement creates mobility

circumference the distance around a circle or sphere

cirrus clouds high, wispy clouds

climatology the study of climate

compression strain on rock that comes from opposite directions

condensation the process of gas turning into liquid

condensation nuclei particles on which water vapor condenses

conductor a substance through which electricity travels

continental divide a ridge that separates rivers flowing in opposite directions on a continent or large land mass

continental margin a name for the area of ocean nearest the continents, including the continental shelf, slope, and rise

continental rise the area of the ocean floor that rises from the abyssal plain to meet the continental slope

continental shelf an underwater land mass extending from a continent

continental shields basement rock that formed the bases of modern-day continents

continental slope the ocean floor that slopes down from the continental shelf to meet the continental rise

convection cell the circular pattern of air currents above Earth that result from different air temperatures

convection current movement of water caused by differences in temperature

corona the bright ring of solar activity visible around the Sun

crater the major opening of a volcano which contains magma and from which lava, gases and volcanic matter generally escape

crest the upper part of a wave

crust the outer sedimentary layer of the planet Earth or other planets; Earth's solid surface

crustacean a marine invertebrate with a hard exterior shell

cumulonimbus clouds cumulus clouds likely to produce precipitation

cumulus clouds tall, puffy, flat-bottomed clouds

cyclone a whirlwind

D

Dalmatian coastline coasts where water seeps inland covering mountain valleys parallel to the shore

deflected current movement of ocean water that changes direction when the water meets a land mass

delta a fan-shaped river outlet made of silt deposits

diameter the measure across a circular plane

divide a ridge of high land that separates rivers flowing one direction from rivers flowing another

ductile deformation permanent shape change of rock due to stress

dunes tall mounds or mountains of sand

E

eclipse when one celestial body partially or completely hides another

elastic deformation when stress on a rock is of short enough duration that the rock returns to its original shape after stress is relieved

elastic limit the boundary after which stress on rock will cause permanent change of shape

elevation the height of a particular location above sea level

ellipse an elongated circle, forming an oval

equator the imaginary line drawn around Earth bisecting it into the Northern and Southern Hemispheres

estuary a flooded mud-plain at the mouth of a river

evaporite deposits solid mineral residue, or leftovers, after evaporation

evolution the process of genetic adaptation to the environment over time

extinction the complete destruction of a species of plant or animal

F

fabricate to create by human production rather than natural processes

fault evidence of shifting plates and released stress of moving solid rock seen by broken crust on Earth's surface

fjards lowland ocean inlets created by glaciers and studded with small islands

flagellum a tail-like object attached to a cell that moves in a whiplike fashion to initiate and sustain mobility

floodplain a low-lying area subject to flooding when the streams or rivers overflow

fracture the break or snap of rock due to unbearable stress

G

glacier a mass of ice that moves across land like a very slow, powerful river

graben a trench created in Earth's surface by faults

gravity the force of attraction between two objects

gravity wave a wave with a period greater than 1/10 of a second and less than 5 minutes

greenhouse effect the inability of heat to escape into Earth's atmosphere

greenstone belts earliest land masses, mostly made of granite

groundwater water retained underground in aquifers

gullet a throat or throatlike channel in an animal

gyre the circular movement of surface currents in an ocean

H

headlands the land masses arcing around a bay of water
hemisphere one half of a sphere
herbivore; herbivorous a plant-eating animal; plant-eating
hominid any of a family of humans
horst a ridge created in Earth's surface by faults
hotspot an area of particularly active magma movement in Earth's mantle
humidity the moisture in the air

I

ice age a period of time when a large proportion of the planet Earth is covered in ice
insolation the energy from the Sun that reaches Earth
invertebrate an animal without internal skeletal structures
ionized carrying a positive or negative electric charge
isobars lines generally forming concentric circles on a weather map indicating different air pressure zones
isotherms lines on a weather map connecting geographic points where air temperature is the same

L

land breeze a cool wind blowing over the ocean from land
lava molten rock (magma) that issues from Earth's surface
load the silt which a river carries
locomotion the ability to move from place to place
longitudinal waves horizontal wave movement through solids or liquids
long wave a wave with a period greater than 5 minutes and less than 12 hours

M

magma molten rock under Earth's surface
mantle the layer under Earth's surface made of rock and molten rock
mares flat surface areas of the Moon
meteor a stone and/or metal mass traveling in the solar system
microscopic so small as to be seen only through great magnification, such as by using a microscope
mineral a compound of elements and chemical reactions
mitosis the process of reproduction by cell division
molecules the smallest independent unit of a compound, or combination, of chemicals
monocline deformation escalator-shaped rock due to stress
mouth the outlet of a stream or river into a larger body of water

N

nimbus clouds clouds likely to precipitate

nocturnal active at night

normal fault a type of fault in which one surface edge travels vertically down another surface edge

nucleus the center of a cell containing DNA, among other substances, enclosed by a membrane

numerical forecasting weather forecasting based on physics and mathematical probabilities

nutrients particles of substances required to sustain life

O

oblique fault a type of fault in which solid rock is moved both vertically and horizontally

obsidian volcanic glass of hardened lava

ocean basin the ocean floor that includes the abyssal plains and ocean ridge

oceanologists people who study oceans, not to be confused with oceanographers, who study the geography of the ocean

ocean ridge the 31,000-mile long part of the ocean floor that resembles a mountain range

orbit the path of a satellite around a celestial body; to travel in a path around a celestial body

organic referring to anything containing chemical compounds of carbon, primarily plant and/or animal

overturn the process by which warmer water at the bottom of a lake or pond is replaced by water cooled at the surface

ozone a form of oxygen in Earth's atmosphere that filters ultraviolet rays from the Sun

P

pelagic sediment ocean floor sediment created from organisms within the ocean

period the measure of the speed of a wave

permeable used to describe a rock with many interconnected pores that is able to release water to the surface

photosynthesis the usually vegetative process of making energy from sunlight, taking in carbon dioxide and releasing oxygen

polar easterlies eastern winds that usually blow at 60° latitude north and south

poles the strongest points of a magnet, which are at either end

porousness the amount of pores, or holes able to contain water, in a rock

precipitate out to separate from liquid into a solid form

primate a member of the group of living creatures that includes apes, humans, and monkeys

prime meridian the imaginary line drawn from the North to South Poles, perpendicular to the equator, which runs through Greenwich, England

R

recumbent deformation folded alteration or shape change of rock due to stress

reverse fault a type of fault in which one surface edge travels vertically up another surface edge

rias coasts where water seeps inland covering mountain valleys perpendicular to the shore

rotate; rotation to spin on one's axis; the act of spinning on one's axis

S

satellite a celestial body in orbit around another celestial body

saturated zone a layer of ground filled to its limit, or saturated, with water

scale the relationship or comparison of sizes

sea breeze a cool wind blowing inland off the ocean

siliceous oozes decayed silica animal shells on the ocean floor

silt particles of sediment carried by rivers and streams

sound a long inlet of water parallel to the shore

source region the surface over which an air mass travels

stationary in a fixed position, unable to move

statistical forecasting weather forecasting based on historical knowledge of weather patterns and mathematical probabilities

storm surges large amounts of ocean water whipped up by hurricane winds

strata layers of the same kind of rock

stratonimbus clouds stratus clouds likely to produce precipitation

stratus clouds clouds in a layer formation

strike-slip fault a type of fracture in Earth's crust in which two plate edges slide past each other

subduction when one tectonic plate moves under another

sublimation the process by which gases turn into solids without first becoming liquid

summer solstice when the Sun's rays fall directly on the Tropic of Cancer (in the Northern Hemisphere, June 21)

sunspots dark shadowy areas visible on the Sun's surface

surf waves breaking on a shore

surface current movement of ocean water caused by winds on the ocean's surface

syncline deformation U-shaped change of rock shape due to stress

synoptic forecasting a method of weather forecasting based on current weather information gathered within a particular region

syzygy the precise alignment, or lineup, of a number of celestial bodies

T

tectonic plate a section of Earth's crust

tension strain that pulls rocks in opposite directions

terrigenous sediment ocean floor sediment that washes down from land

tetrapod an animal with four legs

thermocline the level of water in the ocean where sunlight does not reach and temperatures drop drastically

tides the movement of Earth's surface water resulting from the Moon's and the Sun's gravity

topography geological features on Earth's surface

traits characteristics

transverse waves vertical wave movement through solids or liquids

tributary a stream or small river that contributes water to a larger river

tropical easterlies eastern winds that usually blow at the equator

tsunami an ocean wave created by an earthquake or volcano that reaches great height and speed as it hits land

U

uniform stress strain on rock that comes from all directions

unsaturated zone a layer of ground not saturated or filled to its limit with water

upwelling warm water rising to the surface of a body of water

V

vertebrate an animal with a skeleton or some internal skeletal structure

volcanologist a scientist who studies volcanoes

W

wane to grow smaller; to decrease

wax to grow larger; to increase

westerlies western winds that usually blow at 30° latitude north and south

winter solstice when the Sun's rays fall directly on the Tropic of Capricorn (in the Northern Hemisphere, December 21)

BIBLIOGRAPHY

Asimov, Isaac. *Isaac Asimov's Guide to Earth and Space*. New York: Fawcett Crest, 1991.

Brass, Charles O. *The Essentials of Astronomy*. New Jersey: Research and Education Association, 1995.

Day, John A., and Vincent J. Schaefer. *Peterson First Guides: Clouds and Weather*. Boston: Houghton Mifflin, 1991.

Denecke, Edward J., Jr. *Let's Review: Earth Science*. New York: Barron's Educational Series, 1995.

Dennis, Jerry. *It's Raining Frogs and Fishes*. New York: HarperPerennial, 1992.

Erickson, Jon. *A History of Life on Earth*. New York: Facts on File, 1995.

————— *An Introduction to Fossils and Minerals*. New York: Facts on File, 1992.

————— *The Mysterious Oceans*. Pennsylvania: TAB Books, 1988.

————— *Volcanoes and Earthquakes*. Pennsylvania: TAB Books, 1988.

Lockhart, Gary. *The Weather Companion*. New York: John Wiley & Sons, 1988.

Ojakangas, Richard W. *Introductory Geology*. New York: McGraw Hill, 1991.

The New American Desk Encyclopedia. New York: Meridian, 1994.

Rensberger, Boyce. *How the World Works*. New York: Morrow, 1986.

Seff, Philip, and Nancy R. Seff. *Our Fascinating Earth*. Chicago: Contemporary Books, 1990.

Uvarov, E. B., and Alan Isaacs. *The Penguin Dictionary of Science*. New York: Penguin Books, 1993.

Whitfield, Dr. Philip. *Why Did the Dinosaurs Disappear?* New York: Viking, 1991.

————— *Why Do Volcanoes Erupt?* New York: Viking, 1990.

Whitfield, Dr. Philip, and Joyce Pope. *Why Do the Seasons Change?* New York: Viking, 1987.

Young, John K. *Cells: Amazing Forms and Functions*. New York: Franklin Watts, 1990.

INDEX